Postfeminism, Postrace and Digital Politics in Asian American Food Blogs

This book examines how Asian American women bloggers challenge dominant race and gender discourses through the practice of food blogging.

Asian American food blogs, which situate recipes and food photography within the personal narratives and domestic spaces of Asian American women, offer unique insights into the ways that hegemonic race and gender discourses are negotiated in quotidian life. The genre's focus on food provides a particularly rich backdrop for this study as it necessarily implicates family histories, gendered labour, domestic spaces, and the power dynamics of consumption. These intimate digital texts therefore provide unique insights into the ways that postfeminist and postrace discourses are encountered in the individual's mundane experiences. The author engages a critical cultural analysis of food blogs narratives, images, communities, and platforms expressions of post-race and feminism discourses are constrained by the commercial logics of this digital culture. The author argues that while Asian American food blogs rarely present a sustained challenge to hegemonic identity representation, the processes of reproduction and rupture that define this blogosphere consistently reveal the collective desire to push back against the limits of 'post'-identities.

This is a unique and fascinating study which is ideal reading for students and scholars of gender studies, media studies, cultural studies and sociology.

Tisha Dejmanee is a Lecturer in Digital and Social Media at the University of Technology, Sydney.

Focus on Global Gender and Sexuality

Reading Iraqi Women's Novels in English Translation
Iraqi Women's Stories
Ruth Abou Rached

Gender Hierarchy of Masculinity and Femininity during the Chinese Cultural Revolution
Revolutionary Opera Films
Zhuying Li

Representations of Lethal Gender-Based Violence in Italy Between Journalism and Literature
Femminicidio Narratives
Nicoletta Mandolini

LGBTQI Digital Media Activism and Counter-Hate Speech in Italy
Sara Gabai

Transmasculinity on Television
Patrice A. Oppliger

What Do We Know About the Effects of Pornography After Fifty Years of Academic Research?
Alan McKee, Katerina Litsou, Paul Byron, and Roger Ingham

A Feminist Approach to Sensitive Research
Designing the Clay Embodiment Research Method
Tricia Ong

Postfeminism, Postrace and Digital Politics in Asian American Food Blogs
Tisha Dejmanee

For more information about this series, please visit: https://www.routledge.com/Focus-on-Global-Gender-and-Sexuality/book-series/FGGS

Postfeminism, Postrace and Digital Politics in Asian American Food Blogs

Tisha Dejmanee

LONDON AND NEW YORK

First published 2023
by Routledge
4 Park Square, Milton Park, Abingdon, Oxon OX14 4RN

and by Routledge
605 Third Avenue, New York, NY 10158

Routledge is an imprint of the Taylor & Francis Group, an informa business

© 2023 Tisha Dejmanee

The right of Tisha Dejmanee to be identified as author of this work has been asserted in accordance with sections 77 and 78 of the Copyright, Designs and Patents Act 1988.

All rights reserved. No part of this book may be reprinted or reproduced or utilised in any form or by any electronic, mechanical, or other means, now known or hereafter invented, including photocopying and recording, or in any information storage or retrieval system, without permission in writing from the publishers.

Trademark notice: Product or corporate names may be trademarks or registered trademarks, and are used only for identification and explanation without intent to infringe.

British Library Cataloguing-in-Publication Data
A catalogue record for this book is available from the British Library

Library of Congress Cataloguing-in-Publication Data
Names: Dejmanee, Tisha, author.
Title: Postfeminism, postrace and digital politics in Asian American food blogs / Tisha Dejmanee.
Description: New York, NY : Routledge, 2023. | Series: Focus on global gender and sexuality | Includes bibliographical references and index. |
Identifiers: LCCN 2022034359 (print) | LCCN 2022034360 (ebook) | ISBN 9781032298313 (hardback) | ISBN 9781032298351 (paperback) | ISBN 9781003302278 (ebook)
Subjects: LCSH: Food--Blogs. | Food writing. | Asian American women--United States. | Feminism--United States.
Classification: LCC TX643 .D45 2023 (print) | LCC TX643 (ebook) | DDC 808.06/6641 dc23/eng/20220810
LC record available at https://lccn.loc.gov/2022034359
LC ebook record available at https://lccn.loc.gov/2022034360

ISBN: 978-1-032-29831-3 (hbk)
ISBN: 978-1-032-29835-1 (pbk)
ISBN: 978-1-003-30227-8 (ebk)

DOI: 10.4324/9781003302278

Typeset in Times New Roman
by MPS Limited, Dehradun

To my mother, who always cooked with love.

Contents

Acknowledgements — ix

1 **(Re)producing Postfeminism and Postrace in the Food Blogosphere** — 1
An Introduction to the Food Blogosphere 3
Postfeminism, Postrace and Asian American Food Bloggers 7
The Quotidian Whiteness of the Food Blogosphere 12
Politics and Potential in the Asian American Food Blogosphere 15
The Saveur Blog Awards 18
Chapter Outline 20
Conclusion 21

2 **Asian-Inspired: Branding Race in the Food Blogosphere** — 26
Recipes as Autobiographical Life Writing 27
Containing Race in the Database 30
Self-Branding and Race as Lifestyle Philosophy 36
Authenticity and Cultural Translation 41
Ruptures of Melancholy, Loss, and Anger 44
Conclusion 47

3 **Comments, Community and Controversy: Imagining the Asian American Audience** — 52
The Imagined Community of the Food Blogosphere 54
Imagining Audience through Food Blog Comments 57
Comment Curation on Asian American Food Blogs 60

Desperately Seeking the (Asian American) Audience 64
Conclusion 67

4 **#BlackoutTuesday and Influencer Activism on Instagram**   **74**
The Changing Taste for Race-Based Activism 76
Racial Activism as Brand Strategy 78
Rhetorical Distancing and the Model Minority Myth 82
Conclusion 86

5 **#StopAsianHate and Asian American Activism on Food Blogs**   **91**
The Nascent #StopAsianHate Movement 92
Engaging #StopAsianHate in the Food Blogosphere 95
  Viet World Kitchen 96
  Woks of Life 98
  Nom Nom Paleo 101
Best Practices for Asian American Influencer Activism 102
  Provide History and Context 102
  Make Asian American Communities Visible 103
  Orient Political Awareness Towards Tangible Action and Goals 103
  Actively Champion Black and Minority Solidarity 104
  Sustained Conversations on Social Activism 104
Conclusion 105

6 **Conclusion**   **111**

Appendix   117
Index   119

Acknowledgements

This project has taken shape over a relatively long period of time which means that there are many wonderful people to thank for their support. Deep gratitude goes first to my inspirational dissertation committee members at the University of Southern California, Sarah Banet-Weiser, Aniko Imre, Tara McPherson and Alison Trope whose guidance and mentorship was and continues to be a gift. My Los Angeles community, Peter Enzminger, Michael Raley, Tolian Gjika, Cynthia Wang, Sam Close, Rox Samer, Raffi Sarkissian and the 2011 Annenberg cohort, deeply enriched my graduate student experience and were an encouraging audience for very early versions of this work. My former Communication colleagues at Central Michigan University, who were kind and taught me so much about working life in the academy, and the very special community of friends in Mount Pleasant particularly Britt and Dustin Fremion, Kirsten and Dan Weber, Joe Packer, Zulfia Zaher and Imran Mazid, Lane and Jennifer Demas – and the incredible group of accompanying tiny humans and furry friends – and especially to Rebecca Conklin who provided valuable insights on this manuscript in its final stages. It is meaningful to me that the final version of this manuscript was submitted back in Mount Pleasant. Much appreciation to my current Digital and Social media colleagues at the University of Technology, Sydney, Heather Ford, Francesco Bailo, Paul Byron, Suneel Jethani, Amelia Johns, Natalie Krikowa, Alan McKee and Bhuva Narayan for their support and wonderful companionship and collegiality. Thanks to the Dejmanee family – mum, dad, Nina and Art for their constant support and for providing so much sustenance over the years. To Flemming Rhode, who has journeyed by my side intellectually and through some amazing life adventures, and is a true and cherished partner. Finally, thanks to Anya and Tahlia, my fierce and funny and wonderful ones. In the language of the ARC, you are interruptions. I have never been so grateful to have been interrupted.

1 (Re)producing Postfeminism and Postrace in the Food Blogosphere

Lillian, the Asian American blogger behind the food blog *Chinese Grandma*, begins the biography on her About page with the statement "I'm not a grandma, and this isn't a Chinese food blog", a pair of negative declaratives that give rise to a digital identity through disidentification that stands out within the more typically brash and intentional presentations of self that are published across the food blogosphere. As she goes on to explain, the use of *Chinese Grandma* as her blog's name is a nod to her racial heritage that she re-fashions as a set of personal qualities including thrift, resourcefulness and generosity. In tracing these qualities from her biological grandmas, through to her mother, and then to her circle of Chinese and non-Chinese friends, she presents race as a disembodied commodity that can be transcended, exchanged and adopted by choice. By enfolding her pan-Asian and non-Asian recipes within reflective essays on life, home space and family, Lillian demonstrates the food blogosphere's focus on intimate expressions of work, domesticity, and feminine identity. The result is a digital autobiography that elaborately documents the ways that postrace and postfeminist discourses and their inherent contradictions are navigated within the everyday lives and mundane routines of individual women.

Food blogs have stirred many excited musings from feminist media, cultural studies, and food scholars about their potential for expressing everyday politics, building on a rich body of work on everyday subversion in feminized popular culture and the possibilities for identity play on digital media. In this spirit, the feminist potential of the food blogosphere might be understood through the way these texts grant authorial voice to women, generate diverse representational practices, and center women's quotidian domestic experiences while building communities and creative cultures that are facilitated through the networked structure of digital texts. Yet, the commercial and technological structures which have organized these individual blog narratives and reflections into an established and lucrative genre have also produced a homogeneity among these user-generated texts that, in many instances, amplifies postfeminist and postrace fantasies. This book engages with this tension, documenting the ways in which food blogs are built upon the reproduction of idealized tenets of postfeminist and postrace subjectivity, which has the effect of systematically reducing the potential for bloggers to make unique or radical interventions into representational politics. After all, Lillian specifically invokes her 'real' Chinese grandmas to authorize postrace discourse, not to challenge it, and it is this adherence to dominant racial ideologies that contributes to the visibility and success of her blog.

At the same time, it is true that food blogs are complex and inevitably partial representations of the individual experience. Visibility in the blogosphere is predicated upon regular updates and the endless churning of content. I contend that it is within this process of compulsory reproduction, and within the depths of blog post narratives, that individual bloggers reveal the specific points at which the inherent contradictions of postfeminist and postrace discourses are negotiated. These take place on *Chinese Grandma*, for instance, in posts where Lillian details her nuanced reactions to Amy Chua's 'tiger mom' manifesto and in recipes which allow her to engage with contested issues of authenticity in Chinese American cooking. These moments can be understood as ruptures to the veneer of idealized postfeminist and postrace subjectivity which is generally faithfully reproduced across the blogosphere. While such ruptures are rare, subtle and do not constitute political subversion in and of themselves, they reveal the tenuousness of neoliberal ideology and the individual's continuous negotiation of such in their daily lives. That is, food blogs document individual and mundane, gendered and embodied realities of 'post-' discourse, offering a perspective that is not necessarily the radical or revolutionary re-writing of self through digital tools but an expression of the hopes and contradictions around identity construction that individuals make sense of through their everyday experiences.

In this book, I draw on a sample of Saveur Award-nominated food blogs by Asian American women to document the common strategies through which race and gender are performed in this digital genre, and to identify moments of rupture which momentarily disturb or challenge limited and problematic representations of Asian American femininity. Asian American food bloggers are demographically overrepresented within the predominantly white North American food blogosphere, yet to date there has been a lack of intersectional analyses that draw on specifically Asian American histories and discourses to contextualize race in these media productions. I chart the expression of everyday and more explicit politics across this sample, examining how postfeminist and postrace discourses intersect and work to variously make race and gender visible or invisible. Moreover, I argue that this intersectional approach is significant as an attention to race often modulates arguments about the food blogosphere's feminist potential, particularly as the conventions of this genre discourage honest and critical discussions of how racism impacts the experiences of Asian American women and the commercialization of this genre means that Asian American communities are rarely the imagined audience for this work. This book begins by focusing on the everyday ways in which Asian American food bloggers reproduce and challenge discourses around identity construction through the work of self-branding and community building on their blogs. I then look at the impact of the post-2016 political and activist landscape on the food blogosphere. Cultural events including the rise of hashtag activism, the Trump regime, and the mainstream and commercial attention to Black Lives Matter have fundamentally shifted the political landscape through the emergence of a digital, youth-driven political culture that has embraced radical and political social activism. I discuss the ways in which this shift has impacted the conventions of the food blogosphere which, although originally formulated as an 'apolitical' space, has slowly but surely moved to normalize activism and social justice messages within food blogging practice.

Over the course of this book, what becomes clear is not the radical politics of the food blogosphere but, rather, its malleability which arises as a result of the thoughtful and persistent labors of individual bloggers. In an irrevocably ambivalent political landscape, the food blogosphere demonstrates the necessity of acknowledging the inevitable ways that identity construction is fashioned within the structures of postrace and postfeminism while simultaneously insisting on the individual's continued capacity to question and challenge these structures. This book is a collection of the many ways that Asian American food bloggers have strategically and creatively performed the ideals of postrace, postfeminist subjectivity without losing their ability to critique the failures of these ideals.

An Introduction to the Food Blogosphere

Food blogs are digital media texts that combine recipes and food photography with personal narratives and reflections, and comprise the largest subcategory within the lifestyle blogosphere (Jacob, 2017). Typically, they are authored by individual women and showcase original or adapted recipes that are produced and photographed within the home of the blogger, although many subgenres and variations on this basic format exist including blogs that adopt more of a restaurant critic or travel format; blogs where food posts are integrated with other lifestyle content; and, blogs that are co-authored by multiple bloggers or commercial entities. The rise of food blogs takes place within a period of exponential growth in the production of food media such as cookbooks, food magazines, and food television in the last half-century (Miller, 2007), and the food blogosphere experienced its own surge in the early 21st century (Lofgren, 2013). Given the ephemerality of the blogosphere, it would be futile and perhaps meaningless to try and record the actual numbers of food blogs in existence. However, two important generalizations about food blogs are that they are extremely popular – with one *Medium* article estimating at least 40,000 active food blogs with more than 1000 monthly visitors and a significantly larger pool of less successful food blogs also in circulation (Jain, 2015) – and highly skewed toward female authors and readers (Henry, 2011; Nielsen, 2012; Matchar, 2013). Some early and influential pioneers of the food blogosphere include Julie Powell whose 2002 blog *The Julie/Julia Project* – documenting her attempt to cook all the recipes in Julia Child's *Mastering the Art of French Cooking* (Suthivarakom, 2011) – was popularized by the Hollywood film *Julie & Julia* featuring Amy Adams and Meryl Streep; Ree Drummond who has built a multimillion dollar brand empire around her food blog *The Pioneer Woman*; Deb Perelman, who has blogged since 2006 at *Smitten Kitchen*; and, Molly Wizenberg, whose food blog *Orangette* chronicled her experiments with food after dropping out of a PhD in cultural anthropology and eventually opening a successful restaurant and bar in Seattle. These early experimental and influential texts set the foundation for, and reflect the blogosphere's continuing investment in, documenting the mundane and interior experiences of domestic life from the perspective of white, middle-class, cisgender, North American women.

Given that the food blogosphere is user-generated and ever-evolving, what is surprising is the relative stability and homogeneity of the genre which is a result of the interlocking influences of platform affordances, algorithmic hierarchies of visibility, and commercial logics. Some of the most prominent features of the genre include the emphasis on personal narratives to contextualize recipes, lush and expertly styled food photography referenced colloquially as 'food porn,' the adoption of a cheerful and self-deprecating tone that approximates an assumed intimacy with the unseen audience, and an emphasis on community, with the food blogosphere facilitating many structured and unstructured, on- and offline forums for bloggers and audiences to meet, communicate and build relationships which, although not uniformly supportive, have proven incredibly resonant for some, with many anecdotes of food blog communities providing tangible resources for participants in the form of knowledge exchanges, emotional care, and financial support.

Food blogs center the individual experience, highlighting the ways that food is embedded into the quotidian and mundane through long personal narratives in which memories, daily events, family histories and food tips are shared in the manner of a diary entry. The inclusion of such 'dumb little stories' (as self-described by blogger Lindsay Ostrom) draws on the blogging platform's historical roots in online diary-writing (Siles, 2011) as well as the fragmentary and anecdotal qualities of women's autobiographical writing (Tye, 2010). These qualities that demonstrate the feminist potential of food blogs as sites that showcase individual, lived experiences of the mundane and the domestic that have rarely been given attention in mainstream media, and hint at the potential value of these texts for Asian American women, whose voices and personal experiences are even less likely to be circulated through mainstream cultural texts. However, in addition to fostering strong bonds within the food blogosphere, the intimacy and authenticity of personal narratives have also functioned to transform the food blogosphere into a lucrative word-of-mouth marketing platform. While the early blogosphere was generally described as experimental and amateurish, the monetization of the blogosphere has developed over the past two decades to the point where the food blogosphere is now aligned with commercial lifestyle media through the high production quality of website design, food styling and photography, and recipes. This alignment has led to the development of more creative ways to incorporate sponsorship, advertising, and brand collaboration opportunities into this space. For instance, the food blogosphere's rise in popularity has developed alongside the evolution of 'guerrilla marketing,' an advertising technique which involves covert marketing practices including "product placement, alternative outdoor, word-of-mouth, and consumer-generated approaches" (Serazio, 2013, p. 2). Guerrilla marketing has arisen from the need to reach jaded consumers who have become more and more wary of traditional advertising and, from the perspective of marketers, bloggers' candor and intimacy make them ideal (and relatively cheap) spokespeople for disseminating trusted brand endorsements to a large audience (Daniels, 2012; Matchar, 2013). Even though bloggers are required to disclose paid or sponsored advertising on their blogs, there is an inevitable collapse between performing 'authenticity' versus 'reality advertising' (Pham, 2015). Accordingly, food blogging is now understood as a professional venture that can be monetizable, despite many successful food bloggers continuing with narratives that downplay the professionalism or labor involved in producing a successful food blog. Moreover, even though the majority of blogs do not see significant profits (Daniels, 2012; Matchar, 2013; Pham, 2015), this logic nevertheless underpins the conventions of the food blogging genre, leading to an overwhelming investment in reproducing the normative fantasies of a white, heterosexual, middle-class North American subject and the convention of avoiding controversial or explicit political discussions in this digital culture (Lofgren, 2013).

This book engages with the tensions inherent to this foregrounding of the personal in commercial logics – which renders individuals as brands, friends as followers, intimate narratives as search engine optimization, and knowledge exchanges as valuable commodities – that structure representation in the food blogosphere. While this commercialization does not foreclose the political possibilities of these texts, they structure the ways in which Asian American food bloggers are able to talk about race in this context. For instance, as bloggers of color continue to be denied similar sponsorship opportunities to white bloggers (Daniels, 2012), Asian American food bloggers are often compelled to commodify race and to translate their experiences for an imagined white commercialized following.

Throughout this book, I purposefully acknowledge the sprawl of the food blogosphere by referring to Asian American food bloggers' branded Instagram accounts as part of the food blogosphere, particularly in the final two chapters. These Instagram accounts use the brand names attached to the food blog, are verified accounts that link them to the credibility and digital influence built up through the food blogosphere, and almost exclusively focus on publishing content related to corresponding food blog brands, underlining the use of these accounts as important cross-platform promotional tools that establish the presence of food blogs within social media networks. I would also argue that it is not correct to refer to these accounts as 'Food Instagram,' as this is a genre with its own culture, conventions and leading influencers. While there are platform and genre-specific conventions to blogs and Instagram accounts that are noted in the analysis, this intentional terminology emphasizes the food blogosphere's interconnected, porous and evolving nature, with its meaning and significance spreading beyond individual food blogs.

Postfeminism, Postrace and Asian American Food Bloggers

The food blogosphere is a distinctly postfeminist space with food bloggers embodying the contradictions of postfeminist fantasy through simultaneously adopting a confident capacity about their food work and yet performing girlish self-deprecation of their attempts at domestic perfection; asserting that their food work is a creative, pleasurable choice while also demonstrating their entrepreneurial gumption and the flexibility and resilience of the skilled neoliberal subject. Beginning in the 1990s and continuing in the following decades as a mediated ideology, postfeminism is characterized as a 'double movement' in which "feminism is taken into account, but only to be shown to be no longer necessary" (McRobbie, 2009, p. 17) as select 'fun' tenets of a liberal feminist agenda – such as "sexual freedom, the right to drink, smoke, have fun in the city, and be economically independent" (McRobbie, 2009, p. 12) – have ostensibly been 'achieved,' repudiating any further need for feminism as a political movement (Tasker & Negra, 2007; McRobbie, 2009; Douglas, 2010). Postfeminism results in the "entanglement of both feminist and anti-feminist themes" (Gill, 2007, p. 149), for instance, through an idealized and unattainable female subjectivity that is fun, sexy and glamorous; ambitious, independent and determined; and, most importantly, willingly aligned with a normatively feminine and heterosexual commercial culture. Moreover, postfeminism is typically understood through the nebulous term 'empowerment' – which both assures the profitability of a seductive commodity feminism, while conversely suggesting that any choice made by an individual woman is empowering and thus feminist. This appropriation of feminist qualities champions a feminine subjectivity that imbues certain privileged individuals with strength but presents no threat to patriarchy or the heterosexual matrix, and repudiates the need or possibility for a collective feminist politics. That is, postfeminism is aligned with the imperatives of neoliberalism and a white supremacist, patriarchal agenda.

Postfeminism has been critiqued by numerous feminist theorists who have pointed out the damage wrought by this pseudo-feminist messaging as it undermines a radical, structural political agenda (Gill, 2007; Tasker & Negra, 2007; McRobbie, 2009; Douglas, 2010) and authorizes ever more regressive representations of women (Douglas, 2010).

Criticism has also been directed towards postfeminism's tendency to ignite inter-generational friction by blaming (imagined second-wave) feminists for any dissatisfaction young women may feel (Gill, 2007; McRobbie, 2009; Vavrus, 2012) and accusing feminists who would object to postfeminist sexism of not understanding the irony with which it has been revived and/or simply being old, angry and bitter (Douglas, 2010). While I agree with these feminist critiques, I also seek to attribute greater agency to subjects who have come of age during the heyday of postfeminist ideologies in the 1990s and 2000s. Indeed, while the majority of postfeminist scholarship has focused on mediated representations of postfeminist subjects across a broad array of popular culture – and the limited portrayals dreamed up by mainstream media with vested commercial interests – relatively little postfeminist scholarship has been dedicated to analyzing how individual women have questioned, challenged and rejected postfeminist discourse. Food blogs offer valuable insight in this regard. While food blogs are stylized identity performances that are constrained both by affordances and their own commercial imperatives, they are nevertheless media productions by individual women who have been raised within a dominant postfeminist culture. Food bloggers document the ambivalence with which postfeminist discourse is at once invoked and challenged through lived, mundane experiences and how these contradictory discourses are enfolded in everyday life. That is, food blogs more accurately describe how individual subjects make meaning of postfeminist ideology, often through reproducing fantasized elements of postfeminist citizenship but also through revealing the ruptures that inevitably occur as a result of the inherent contradictions of this identity performance.

Several scholars have laid foundations for the study of food blogs as postfeminist texts. Rodney, Cappeliez, Oleschuk and Johnston (2017) document how femininity is performed in the food blogosphere through the presentation of homemade meals, the pleasures of self-care, and harnessing appetites, which all involve contradictions that are reconciled by bloggers through a process of calibration. Paula M Salvio draws on pioneering food blogs including *Orangette, Smitten Kitchen* and *The Pioneer Woman* to argue that the blogosphere amplifies postfeminist sensibilities by "exacerbat[ing] distinctions between men and women and provok[ing] middle-class anxieties about having children, finding a husband, and securing the comforts of home" (2012, p. 35). Alane Presswood describes how food blogs embody postfeminist contradiction, representing "*both* a form of increased agency and vital community-building for women, *and* a harmful reinforcing of gender, race, and class-based hierarchies" (2020, p. 8).

While I build on this documentation of the postfeminist spirit that is captured by the food blogosphere, I seek to more explicitly foreground how race intersects with these gendered performances, specifically for Asian American food bloggers.

The centering of white, heterosexual, middle-class girls and women is a feature of postfeminist media and theory (McRobbie, 2009; Butler, 2013; Projansky, 2014) and coincides with the construction of aspirational consumer citizenship in mainstream commercial culture. However, Jess Butler points out that the "tendency to conceptualize postfeminism as primarily exclusionary obscures the ways in which this discursive formation *includes* (albeit in specific and limited ways) nonwhite and nonheterosexual subjects" (2013, pp. 48–49). In a similar fashion Simidele Dosekun criticizes the presumed Eurocentrism of postfeminist discourses, focusing on Nigerian subjects to argue that postfeminism "hails and welcomes into its fold diverse and distanciated subjects who have the material, discursive, and imaginative capital to *buy into it*" (2020, p. 5). Several scholars have responded to the call to broaden the inquiry of postfeminist subjectivity to non-white subjects, with research into the Asian postfeminist subject including Michelle Bae's (2011) research on how a Korean teen girl's image-making practices work to disrupt notions of postfeminist girl power, and Tony Tran's (2020) discussion of the work of Anti-Phans who critique Asian American YouTuber Michelle Phan as a way of negotiating postfeminist standards of beauty. This book continues this study of Asian American food bloggers as postfeminist subjects working within an inherently white digital food blogging culture and compelled by commercial and postrace imperatives to strategically erase and commodify their racial identities.

While food blogs actively and prominently forward exaggerated and hypervisible representations of gender through idealized postfeminist citizenship, postrace discourse functions concurrently to obfuscate the discussion or visibility of race in this digital culture. Postrace discourse is a dominant ideology in the US where, in the place of explicitly racist laws and policies, a white racial order is instead maintained through rhetorics of colorblindness and meritocracy that attribute success to individual perseverance and 'good choices' while systematically denying the continued impact of structural racism on people of color (Bonilla-Silva, 2003; Joseph, 2018). Obama's presidency marked an ascendant moment for postrace discourse, with many leaning on the fact that a Black man could be elected to the highest office in the country as ostensible evidence that race was no longer a barrier to success or positive social outcomes (Ladson-Billings & Tate, 2016;

Joseph, 2018). Furthermore, Ladson-Billings & Tate (2016) and Ono (2010) point out that this narrative of postracial triumph has been equally popular with conservatives and liberals, with postrace discourse sharing ideological foundations with the seemingly liberal terms of 'multiculturalism' and 'racial tolerance.' Postrace ideology results in vehement opposition to State policies that are designed to address the continuing, long-term impacts of racism such as affirmative action, and instead puts faith in the 'corrective' measures of individual choice and meritocracy to explain and maintain the social order. In this context, explicitly racist policies and discourse are replaced by a 'new racism' that flourishes in ways that are subtle, institutional and seemingly non-racial (Bonilla-Silva, 2015).

Postrace discourse shares several key characteristics with postfeminism. Both are reliant on historical revisionism and repudiation which suggests that racism and sexism are problems that have been resolved, and those wishing to continue to talk about such issues are the cause of discontent. The myths of postrace and postfeminism are both upheld through the hypervisibility of exemplary individuals – typically, female and Black celebrities and figureheads – who are able to support the idea that individuals no longer face social barriers and, instead, individual qualities and choices are the primary determinants of social success. These logics of neoliberal individualism work to dismantle collective political formations, and result in a political silencing which for the postfeminist subject is understood as "withholding of critique [as] a condition of her freedom" (McRobbie, 2009) or, in postrace society, manifests as an extreme discomfort in talking about race in any capacity (Bonilla-Silva, 2003). This political silencing allows regressive sexism and racism to flourish (Bonilla-Silva, 2003; Douglas, 2010) while simultaneously, and perversely, triggering the rise of explicitly racist and anti-feminist backlash movements.

This invisibilization of race for Asian American food bloggers is further compounded by the fact that postrace is most often articulated through the dominant Black-white binary of US race relations and history. Indeed, in Bonilla-Silva's (2003) surveys, respondents often pointed to individuals of Asian descent as examples to support their postrace fallacies, typically in reference to the model minority myth. The model minority myth remains the dominant narrative for framing the Asian American community in the US, attributing the supposed success of Asian American immigrants to their strong work ethic and respect for authority to succeed at work and educational opportunities (Ono & Pham, 2009; Kim & Taylor, 2017). While ostensibly lauding the Asian American community, the model minority myth in fact functions to support white supremacy through political rhetoric that acts as a "controlling and divisive mechanism for people of color" (Kim & Taylor, 2017, p. 2) pitting Asian Americans against Black Americans and other racial minorities (Ono & Pham, 2009; Kim & Taylor, 2017). Meanwhile, the model minority myth continues to enact harm for the Asian American community as it has "silenced Asian Americans against racism, maintained the *status quo*, and challenged the mental health of Asian Americans" (Kim & Taylor, 2017, p. 2) while also failing to recognize the large discrepancies in socioeconomic status and education levels within the Asian American community (Nakamura, 2002). Moreover, the alleged honor of model minority status is conditional and precarious. Kent Ono and Vincent Pham point out that while the model minority myth is superficially seen to displace 'yellow peril' discourse – which [highlights] the apparently imminent threat of "Asians and Asian Americans ... to take over, invade, or otherwise negatively Asianize the US nation and its society and culture" (Ono & Pham, 2009, p. 25) – in fact, the model minority myth shares continuities with yellow peril discourse as it posits that "Asians and Asian Americans who have become successful in fact pose a looming threat to the US nation-state" (Ono & Pham. 2009, p. 81). As will be examined through the course of this book, when social and political conditions shift, the conditional acceptance of Asian Americans within US society can be swiftly revoked.

The current study of Asian American food bloggers is situated within these gaps, elaborating on the specific ways that Asian American women construct identity within the intersecting discourses of postfeminism and postrace, and the conventions of the food blogosphere. My contention is that postfeminist and postrace discourses operate to erase race for Asian American food bloggers, making hypervisible their gendered experiences as aspirational and universal – seeming evidence of their exemplary assimilation and model minority status – while simultaneously affording the possibility for race to be portrayed only in terms of a commodity or positive marker of exotic difference. In turn, this impacts the politics of Asian American food blogs. Specifically, the feminist potentialities of food blogging – including the representational politics of digital self-representation and authorial capacity, the ability to build community, and the focus on the ways that identity politics are inscribed through mundane and domestic life – become far less cogent when applied intersectionally to the experiences of Asian American women bloggers.

The Quotidian Whiteness of the Food Blogosphere

To contextualize the racial politics of Asian American food bloggers it is necessary to understand their work as situated within a food blogosphere that is constructed around the norms of an idealized white, middle-class, heterosexual, cisgender, North American female subject. Throughout this book, I reference this hegemonic positioning when using terms such as 'women' and 'femininity,' acknowledging that while gender is a more expansive concept as well as the presence of male food bloggers, the culture and commercialism of the food blogosphere reinforces and privileges a binary understanding of gender and exaggerated stereotypes of femininity. In a similar fashion, the dominant whiteness of the food blogosphere is related but not equivalent to 'lack of representation' as, given how vast and porous this user-generated space is it is of course possible to find popular and successful examples of food blogs created by people of color. Food blog audiences also selectively engage and curate their own blogospheres, some of which may be overpopulated by diversity that reflect the individual's own interests and subject positioning. However, when exploring the food blogosphere as a cultural phenomenon, it is relevant to understand the blogosphere not as an index of blogs but as a site structured by flows of power that are governed by the rules of visibility and profits in a digital attention economy. For this reason, it is relevant to understand the food blogosphere through the most visible and successful blogs which, due to the hierarchical structure of digital visibility and algorithms, accrue significantly more influence in determining the conventions and significance of this digital culture.

The claim that the food blogosphere is a predominantly feminized and white space is not a statement on demographics so much as it is about the normative ideologies that give the food blogosphere its meaning. While femininity in the food blogosphere flourishes through particularly traditional and girlish depictions of domesticity and heterosexuality – in ways that exaggerate the visibility of gender in this space – dominant whiteness is marked by an invisibility which reflects what Dyer has famously described as the manner that "white power secures its dominance by seeming not to be anything in particular" (2010, p. 44). Given such invisibility, the dominance of whiteness that is normalized and idealized within the food blogosphere can be inferred through contextualizing the histories that give meaning to this genre.

The food blogosphere proliferates white discourse through reifying an uncomplicated relationship to house and land that has roots in white nationalism. This can be seen through the coupling of food blogs to farm ownership, popularized through food blog archetype *The Pioneer Woman* in which Drummond builds her franchise through delineating binaries between urban and ranch life that romanticize a white settler colonial history. This romanticization of farmland is exaggerated through Drummond's references to pioneer life and descriptions of her husband – whom she calls The Marlboro Man – as a seventh-generation farmer. Drummond's recipes, heavily centered around the Standard American Diet of meat and potatoes, provide not just food pedagogies but a lifestyle manual in which the pairing of traditional femininity with the focus on the family home in conservative, regional America leads to the celebration of a nostalgic heartland culture in which women "are tasked with defending, maintaining and perpetuating White culture" (Dejmanee, 2019, p. 81) in a trope that is repeated across the food blogosphere as well as in popular Food Network television shows. Even when not literally set on farms, food blogs overwhelmingly celebrate the suburban home through their attention to glamorous and tastefully renovated kitchen spaces, the activities and events of a cast of family members, and the imagined pleasures of the female subject within the home and nuclear family. Such settings reify the suburban home, rooted in whiteness from its initial conception in Levittown, Pennsylvania, where houses were only sold to white residents (Galyean, n.d.) and continued over the years through the insidious racism of white flight, redlining, discriminatory lending practices, and urban design (Bonilla-Silva, 2003).

Food blogs also allude to nostalgic white suburbia through romanticizing the gendered domesticity of 1950s, post-war America. In this era, domestic appliances revolutionized the home and gave rise to home economics as a scientific endeavor, seemingly professionalizing reproductive labor as part of the technological revolution that promoted women's return to the home as American men returned from fighting abroad (Shapiro, 1986). While 20th century feminists railed against this domestication – most notably through the popularization of Betty Friedan's *The Feminine Mystique* which articulated the internal dissatisfaction of educated, married, middle-class, white women who were bound to their suburban housewife lives – it is also worth recalling bell hooks' insightful critique of this universalization of white women's experiences and desires as the basis for a feminist movement, and the way this second wave tome intentionally overlooked "poor and working class women [who] knew from their experiences that work was neither personally fulfilling nor liberatory – that it was for the most part exploitative and dehumanizing" (hooks, 1984, p. 97). This attention to middle-class whiteness is repeated in the food blogosphere as food blogging is celebrated as a creative, entrepreneurial pursuit when practiced by middle-class, married women but when undertaken by a queer single mom such as British austerity blogger Jack Monroe, decried as a waste of time that should not be a substitute for undertaking paid public sphere work. The assumption of food blogging's whiteness is further indicated by the systematic invisibility of Black food bloggers, who are less likely to be incorporated into commercial sponsorship programs (Daniels, 2012) and are noticeably absent from – or in later years, minimally represented in – Saveur's taste-making food blog awards.

Additionally, whiteness is invoked through the performance of a cultivated 'girlie' femininity as food bloggers adopt a uniquely saccharine feminine persona described as "no serious conflict, no controversy, no cynicism, no snark" (Fortini, 2011) that reinforces the cultural symbolism of white girlhood as representative of purity and innocence. For instance, a girlie femininity is indicated both through the focus on dainty finger foods and sweet baked treats (Inness, 2001; Carroll, 2013; Lofgren, 2013) the global 'cupcake craze' of the 1990s and early 2000s (Nathanson, 2015); the pleasures of food and eating; and, food trends such as 'unicorn food' and the investment in cuteness which is "deeply associated with the infantile and the feminine" (Ngai, 2005, p. 814). While admittedly contemporary iterations of cuteness have a particular relationship to Japanese culture (Yano, 2013), sweet girlishness is connected to whiteness through its evocation of the innocence that is attributed to childhood and historically related to the paternalistic protection of white women, and from which Black women and children are excluded (Lipsitz, 1998). It is also supported through manifestations of girlpower and the girl as a cultural zeitgeist which are largely centered around representations of white girlhood (Harris, 2004; Projansky, 2014).

Against this digital backdrop of dominant whiteness, successful Asian American food bloggers tend to both assimilate as exemplary cultural intermediaries and distinguish themselves by using their racial identities as a unique marker for their brands, referencing Asian family histories and recipes that affirm their authenticity and authority to publish Asian recipes. For instance, Cynthia Chen McTernan describes the food on her blog, *Two Red Bowls*, as "comfort food, and easy, with occasional Asian influences from my Chinese background and [my husband's] Korean mother, and a touch of Southern here and there from my childhood in South Carolina" (ref), a description of Chinese and Korean heritage as a creative influence that can be drawn upon 'occasionally' and by choice, and an identity marker of the same quality as hailing from the South, deemphasizing the history and significance of race in all these identities. This calculated use of race as part of the blogger's brand strategy is ideal for capitalizing on the high value placed on Asian recipes in contemporary foodie culture, which Josee Johnston and Shyon Baumann describe as often practiced through "a hunger for exploring ethnic cuisines" (2010, p. 20) and the quest for authentically presented regional foods. This positioning captures the spirit of model minority subjectivity, preferring color-blindness, aside for moments where racial difference is presented in positive terms or in recognition of its value as a commodity that caters to the prevailing tastes of the imagined white foodie. To point this out is not to place blame on individual Asian American food bloggers but, rather, to note the limitations of the white food blogosphere in supporting meaningful discussion of racial identity politics for the Asian American community.

Politics and Potential in the Asian American Food Blogosphere

The setting for this study spans from the heyday of food blogging in 2009 – long enough after its experimental early days at the beginning of the 21st century that a critical mass had begun to participate as well as to formalize and commercialize this blogosphere's generic conventions, and that such work had begun to be taken seriously by a prestigious mainstream food media outlet such as Saveur – to 2021, a period of significant shifts in the political and digital landscapes including the rise of large, identity-based hashtag activist movements such as #BlackLivesMatter, which originated in 2013, the turn to 'popular feminism' in 2014 (Banet-Weiser, 2018), and the moment of shock for liberals in the wake of Trump's election in 2016. This book charts how Asian American food bloggers have been enfolded in and responded to these cultural moments, beginning with a focus on the food blogosphere's potential to enact representational politics and moving to analyze the ways in which more established social movement actions have been integrated into these branded platforms.

Successful Asian American food bloggers amass sizeable platforms that allow them to challenge representations and stereotypes of the 'model minority.' In response to the crude gendered and raced stereotypes produced in mass media, Asian American food bloggers perform everyday subversion by showcasing an Asian American femininity that is individualized and nuanced. Food blogs give voice to Asian American women and a context to their food work, and the gendered and raced negotiations that take place within their daily domestic and private lives. At the same time, the commercial underwriting of the food blogosphere strains arguments about the everyday politics of the blogosphere, as these logics normalize and glamorize a lifestyle that is predominantly white, middle-class, and heteronormative, actively rewarding those who are able to most faithfully reproduce user-generated versions of hegemonic postfeminist whiteness, *some of whom* are Asian. These logics work to amplify rather than resist hegemonic reproduction, and have reconfigured food blogging as an increasingly professional and elitist venture, with high standards for *visibility*, if not entry. Such facts justify concerns about the limited democratic potential of digital media, and the particular barriers to countering postrace discourse through this genre.

Moreover, while I agree with Presswood's (2020) assessment that food blogging amplifies privileged voices at the expense of marginalized communities, focusing only on the relative social privilege of Asian American food bloggers also threatens to obfuscate the extent to which they continue to be subjects of racism even within the blogosphere itself. For instance, in 2017 a segment from Drummond's *The Pioneer Woman* Food Network show featured the food blogger preparing a batch of 'Asian' chicken wings (only identifiable as 'Asian' through the baffling inclusion of plum jelly and soy sauce) as a practical joke that affirms the flourishing legacy of yellow peril discourse in Western media. As Drummond presents these wings to her cowboy husband and friends, they wrinkle their noses in disgust and say they 'don't trust them' before Drummond gleefully reveals the 'real' Buffalo chicken wings she has prepared, saying she 'wouldn't do that to them' (Morabito, 2017). Despite the healthy representation of Asian American food bloggers, and their ample qualifications to comment on this racist food segment in the scope of their professional work, there was no response to this incident within the food blogosphere. This silence was likely a function of the commercial realities and power dynamics of food blogging, where Asian American food bloggers were unlikely to publicly criticize highly influential Drummond for fear of repercussions to their own blogging brands. More broadly, this example indicates the reluctance to use intimate food blog narratives to share negative experiences of race or racism that might challenge white hegemony or invoke white guilt.

This exploration of Asian American food bloggers' engagement with postrace discourse must be further contextualized through an understanding of how race is imbricated in and through digital technologies. Early techno-utopian accounts of the ways that cyberspace might potentially liberate humans from physical identity markers have been critiqued and largely rejected (e.g. Kolko et al., 2000; Daniels, 2009; Noble & Roberts, 2019). This is especially true as many online environments have become more anchored (Zhao et al., 2008) as well as visual (Daniels, 2009), confirming the normative assumption of whiteness in cyberspace (Brock, 2012) while also making increasingly apparent that identity characteristics such as race cannot simply be discarded, 'tried on', or easily obfuscated in most online interactions (Nakamura, 2002). Accordingly, it is important to consider the various ways that race is coproduced with and as a technology (Kolko et al., 2000), and more recent work has focused on the specific ways that race and racial inequalities are encoded within platforms, algorithms, and the seeming invisibility or omniscience of the digital (Noble, 2018; Benjamin, 2019; Brock, 2012). In the following chapters, I consider the limitations and impacts of blogging architecture and interfaces in the production of race, and how features such as blogging networks, menus, comments, and posts facilitate or hinder dialogue about race and the formation of Asian American community within the food blogosphere.

One of the key features of the food blogosphere is its reliance on content churning, which Julie Wilson and Emily Yochim (2017) describe, in relation to the 'mamasphere,' as the constant updates, endless flows and unrelenting streams of content that constitute the digital mundane. In the food blogosphere, content churning leads Asian American bloggers to constantly perform and reproduce postfeminist and postrace discourses which are strategically perpetuated as digital visibility. At the same time, this continuous, compulsory reproduction opens spaces and possibilities for the inevitable failures of such discourses. That is, while Asian American food bloggers strategically perform an aspirational whiteness and postfeminist subjectivity, it is through doing so that they inevitably reveal and grapple with the contradictions and limitations of postrace and postfeminist ideologies, typically identified as moments of 'rupture' within the churning content production of the blogosphere. Thus, rupture is used as an analytical approach to the pervasive political ambivalence of the Asian American food blogosphere. First, Asian American food bloggers' engagement with postfeminist and postrace discourses is analyzed as a project that requires continuous reproduction for its legibility, both in the performance of identity as well as in the capitalist logics that compel bloggers to publish regularly. Second, within these processes of continuity, I point out the inevitable moments of rupture that take place within the food blogosphere which reveal both the extent to which food blogs are typically aligned with the reproduction of hegemonic ideologies and the specific ways in which food bloggers may resist or challenge such ideologies. Given that the food blogosphere is built upon the repetition and reproduction of formulaic conventions, ruptures signify the moments at which a meaningful and often purposeful deviation from the reproduction of hegemonic ideologies occur and give insight into the political potential and limits of such media representations.

The Saveur Blog Awards

This study is drawn from an archive of finalists of the Saveur Blog Awards between 2009 (its founding year) and 2019. The Saveur Blog Awards are prestigious within the food blogosphere with winners including food blog celebrities such as Ree Drummond, David Lebovitz, Deb Perelman, Mimi Thorisson and Molly Yeh. Any individual, including bloggers and readers, can nominate or self-nominate a blog for consideration, with finalists and winners assessed by a committee at Saveur and, in later years, a winner also determined by popular vote which, revealingly, rarely correlates with the committee's choice. The awards are highly competitive: as a guide, 40,000 nominations were received in 2011 (Saveur, 2011) and 16,000 in 2019 (Saveur, 2019). The structure of the awards has changed over the decade in question with some categories included in more recent years (e.g. 'best food Instagram' and 'best entertaining blog') and some excised (e.g. 'best humor blog' and 'best kitchen tools and hardware coverage'). The categories themselves are informative of limited gendered and racial logics, with the category 'Most Inspired Weekend Dinners' invoking the gendered binary notion of the domestic cook versus the expert chef, and the category 'Best Regional Cuisine Blog' grouping blogs on Cajun, Southern, Texan, Indian, Filipino, Thai food together.

I refined this list of finalists to remove blogs that were no longer visible and blogs that did not focus primarily on recipes and food writing within the domestic space, for instance restaurant review blogs, interior design and entertaining blogs, and food photography blogs with no accompanying narratives. From this sample, I identified blogs that were authored by Asian women by cross-referencing information including their names, photographs, information from their biographies, information from posts, and media interviews. While this is not necessarily a foolproof method for determining race, given the reliance on such information for branding and presenting an authentic and anchored digital identity, in practice such information was readily discernible. I further refined this list to incorporate bloggers that are or have previously been located in North America, including Canada and the US due to the similarities with which the model minority myth hails Asian Americans within these white settler colonialist societies, although admittedly the cultural analysis is more focused on the US political landscape. This process resulted in a sample of 30 blogs – detailed in the Appendix – from which most of the findings in this book are based. While I would not consider this sample to be representative of the food blogosphere as a whole, it does represent a set of very successful Asian American food blogs. Given the hierarchical visibility of the food blogosphere, and the further attention and success accorded to these blogs through their status as Saveur award finalists, this sample constitutes a highly influential sample of food blogs authored by Asian American women.

I employ a multimethodological approach to analyzing these texts. I perform critical cultural interpretation by contextualizing food blogs within broader sociocultural, political and economic systems and draw on an intersectional feminist media studies approach to consider the multiple and overlapping impacts of race and gender, focusing on the histories of racial and gendered relations that inform contemporary Asian American women's subjectivity. While my focus is primarily on food blogs authored by Asian American women, the food blogosphere is porous and connected to a broader cultural context for meaning. Accordingly, I have included references to and analysis of related cultural artifacts, including food blogs by non-Asian authors, lifestyle blogs, mainstream media texts, and digital food texts that are not blogs. In the final two chapters, where my focus moves to food bloggers' participation in hashtag activism, I expand my inquiry to the Instagram accounts associated with the blog sample, as a platform that has been readily adopted by bloggers for both cross-promotion and political discourse. In these chapters, I perform thematic analyses of social media posts to inform my discussion and findings. The reproduction of online material in this book takes into account the Association of Internet Researcher's (AoIR) ethical guidelines and particularly the user's intentions and imagined reach of online material. Given their high public profiles and visibility, content from food bloggers' blogs and Instagram accounts are cited throughout this book. Where blog comments are cited, usernames and links are provided as these comment profiles are rarely linked to anchored identity information. Where racist Instagram comments are cited in Chapter 4, account handles are removed to afford some degree of privacy but it was important to reproduce, rather than paraphrase, these comments in their original form.

Chapter Outline

In the first two chapters of this book, I explore the everyday politics of food bloggers' strategic engagement with postrace and postfeminist discourses. Chapter One focuses on the specific ways that race is stylized within the self-branding strategies of Asian American food bloggers, for instance, as a personal makeover project, a set of mutable personal characteristics, and an authentic commodity that can be translated by food bloggers. While these digital self-representations offer a counternarrative to the most limited mainstream stereotypes of Asian American women, I explore how they nevertheless foreclose the possibility for explicit discussions of racism or social injustice. In Chapter Two, I explore the communities generated on and through food blogs. Drawing on bloggers' patterns of responding to and moderating blog comments, I explore the kinds of dialogue and subject positioning that arise from the Asian American food blogger's imagined audience and the limits to formation of Asian American community as a result of this commercialized following. These two chapters reflect on the everyday ways that bloggers engage, and at times push back against, the ideals of postrace, postfeminist discourses in their online work and identity performances.

In the final two chapters, I examine how the food blogosphere responds to a larger structural and social shift in the conceptualization of digital politics, as hashtag activism gains widespread momentum and identity movements such as #MeToo and Black Lives Matter work in conjunction with cultural shifts to promote more outspoken and mainstream attention to feminism and racial justice. I explore the ways that Asian American food bloggers respond to the subsequent imperatives of influencer activism in Chapter Three, with particular attention to this community's response to #BlackOutTuesday on Instagram. I find that while activism and allyship is earnestly embraced by this community, there continues to be a distancing within this action that prevents Asian American food bloggers from speaking candidly about the ways in which structural racism impacts them and the Asian American community. I complement this study with the exploration of #StopAsianHate in Chapter Four which as a movement focuses more specifically on dispelling the model minority myth and highlighting the continued threat of violence faced by the Asian American community. This action generates far less participation from

Asian American food bloggers, and the food blogosphere as a whole. However, I draw inspiration from the case studies of three Asian American food bloggers – and their deep engagement with race and activist content – and draw on these examples as the basis for articulating best practice guidelines for Asian American influencer activism.

Conclusion

The food blogosphere's popularity and longevity is intimately tied to its potential to be monetized, and over the last two decades, the genre's conventions have been formalized through commercial logics. This underwriting of the food blogosphere has shaped the possibilities for visibility and representation in this site, which is particularly true for Asian American food bloggers who tend to demonstrate a faithful reproduction of postrace and postfeminist discourses on their blogs. While this might seem to be a disappointing concession to the power of the algorithm to reinscribe pre-existing social hierarchies in digital cultures – and these hierarchies are definitely worthy of scrutiny – as Jill Walker Rettberg reminds us,

> to really understand blogs, you need to read them over time. Following a blog is like getting to know someone ... There's a very different sense of rhythm and continuity when you follow a blog, or a group of blogs, over time.
> (2014, p. 4)

I would add that it is through tracking food blogs over time, and charting their continuous processes of discursive reproduction, that ruptures inevitably occur that make clear the limits of postrace and postfeminist identity.

Ultimately, this study of Asian American food bloggers supports the notion of a malleable blogosphere, one that never rejects the guiding principles of hegemonic discourse but continually reflects on and makes visible its contradictions through moments of rupture. Ruptures may be indicated by fleeting moments of willful departure from the conventions, or posts that momentarily drop the cheery food blogger's façade to acknowledge the pain and violence of postrace subjectivity. Ruptures are the stirrings of potential and change, even though in and of themselves they are not political. In the following chapter, I document such ruptures as they emerge in a variety of ways within the Asian American food blogosphere.

References

Bae, M. S. (2011). Interrogating girl power: Girlhood, popular media, and postfeminism. *Visual Arts Research, 37*(2), 28–40. 10.5406/visuartsrese.37.2.0028

Banet-Weiser, S. (2018). *Empowered: Popular feminism and popular misogyny.* Duke University Press.

Benjamin, R. (2019). *Race after technology: Abolitionist tools for the new Jim code.* Polity.

Bonilla-Silva, E. (2003). *Racism without racists: Color-blind racism and the persistence of racial inequality in America.* Rowman & Littlefield.

Bonilla-Silva, E. (2015). The structure of racism in color-blind, "post-racial" America. *American Behavioral Scientist, 59*(11), 1358–1376. 10.1177/0002764215586826

Brock, A. (2012). From the Blackhand side: Twitter as a cultural conversation, *Journal of Broadcasting & Electronic Media, 56*(4), 529–549. 10.1080/08838151.2012.732147

Butler, J. (2013). For white girls only?: Postfeminism and the politics of inclusion. *Feminist Formations, 25*(1), 35–58. 10.1353/ff.2013.0009.

Carroll, A. (2013). *Three squares: The invention of the American meal.* Basic Books.

Daniels, J. (2009). *Cyber racism: White supremacy online and the new attack on civil rights.* Rowman & Littlefield.

Daniels, J. (2012). BlogHer and Blogalicious: Gender, race, and the political economy of women's blogging conferences. In R. Gajjala & Y. J. Oh (Eds.), *Cyberfeminism 2.0* (pp. 29–60). Peter Lang Publishers.

Dejmanee, T. (2019). The Food Network's heartland kitchens: Cooking up neoconservative comfort in the United States. *Critical Studies in Television, 14*(1), 74–89. 10.1177/1749602018810923

Dosekun, S. (2020). *Fashioning postfeminism: Spectacular femininity and transnational culture.* University of Illinois Press.

Douglas, S. (2010). *Enlightened sexism: The seductive message that feminism's work is done.* Times Books.

Dyer, R. (2010). *White: Essays on race and culture.* Routledge.

Fortini, A. (2011, May 2). O pioneer woman! *The New Yorker.* https://www.newyorker.com/magazine/2011/05/09/o-pioneer-woman

Galyean, C. (n.d.) Levittown: The imperfect rise of the American Suburbs. U.S. History Scene. https://ushistoryscene.com/article/levittown/

Gill, R. (2007). Postfeminist media culture: Elements of a sensibility. *European Journal of Cultural Studies, 10*(2), 147–166. 10.1177/1367549407075898

Harris, A. (2004). *Future girl: Young women in the twenty-first century.* Routledge.

Henry, S. (2011). So you want to be a successful food blogger? Here's how. *KQED.* https://www.kqed.org/bayareabites/27706/so-you-want-to-be-a-successful-food-blogger-heres-how

hooks, b. (1984). *Feminist theory: From margin to center*. South End Press.
Inness, S. A. (2001). *Dinner roles: American women and culinary culture*. University of Iowa.
Jacob, D. (2017, June 6). Why BlogHer food ended, after 8 years. *Dianne Jacob – Will Write for Food*. https://diannej.com/2017/blogher-food-ended-after-8-years/
Jain, A. (2015, September 29). What does it take to make your food blog a success? *Medium*. https://medium.com/cucumbertown-magazine/what-it-takes-to-make-your-food-blog-a-success-5c0509ee121a
Johnston, J., & Baumann, S. (2010). *Foodies: Democracy and distinction in the gourmet foodscape*. Routledge.
Joseph, R. L. (2018). *Postracial resistance: Black women, media, and the uses of strategic ambiguity*. New York University Press. 10.2307/j.ctv12pnrm2
Kim, E. H., & Taylor, K. A. (2017). The model minority stereotype as a prescribed guideline of empire: Situating the model minority research in the postcolonial context, *Journal of Southeast Asian American Education and Advancement*, *12*(2). 10.7771/2153-8999.1156
Kolko, B. E., Nakamura, L., & Rodman, G. B. (2000). *Race in cyberspace*. Routledge.
Ladson-Billings, G., & Tate, W. (2016). *Covenant keeper: Derrick Bell's enduring education legacy*. Peter Lang.
Lipsitz, G. (1998). *The possessive investment in whiteness: How white people profit from identity politics*. Temple University Press.
Lofgren, J. M. (2013). *Changing tastes in food media: A study of recipe sharing traditions in the food blogging community*. [Masters by Research thesis, Queensland University of Technology]. QUT ePrints.
Matchar, E. (2013). *Homeward bound: Why women are embracing the new domesticity*. Simon & Schuster.
McRobbie, A. (2009). *The aftermath of feminism: Gender, culture and social change*. SAGE.
Miller, T. (2007). *Cultural citizenship: Cosmopolitanism, consumerism, and television in a neoliberal age*. Temple University Press.
Morabito, G. (2017, March 7). Maybe food network should pull this racist 'Pioneer Woman' episode. *Eater*. https://www.eater.com/2017/3/7/14846788/pioneer-woman-racist-asian-hot-wings
Nakamura, L. (2002). *Cybertypes: Race, ethnicity, and identity on the Internet*. Routledge.
Nathanson, E. (2015). Sweet sisterhood: Cupcakes as sites of feminized consumption and production. In E. Levine (Ed.), *Cupcakes, Pinterest, and Ladyporn* (pp. 249–268). University of Illinois Press. 10.5406/j.ctt16wdkp7.17
Ngai, S. (2005). The cuteness of the avant-garde. *Critical Inquiry*, *31*(4), 811–847. 10.1086/444516
Nielsen. (2012, 8 March). Buzz in the blogosphere: Millions more bloggers and blog readers. *Nielsen*. http://www.nielsen.com/us/en/insights/news/2012/buzz-in-the-blogosphere-millions-more-bloggers-and-blog-readers

Noble, S. (2018). *Algorithms of oppression: How search engines reinforce racism.* New York University Press. 10.18574/9781479833641

Noble, S. U., & Roberts, S. T. (2019). Technological elites, the meritocracy, and postracial myths in Silicon Valley. In R. Mukherjee, S. Banet-Weiser, & H. Gray (Eds.), *Racism Postrace* (pp. 113–130). Duke University Press. 10.1515/9781478003250-007

Ono, K. A. (2010). Postracism: A theory of the 'post-' as political strategy. *Journal of Communication Inquiry, 34*(3), 227–233.

Ono, K. A., & Pham, V. N. (2009). *Asian Americans and the media.* Polity.

Pham, M. H. T. (2015). *Asians wear clothes on the Internet: Race, gender, and the work of personal style blogging.* Duke University Press.

Presswood, A. L. (2020). *Digital domestics: Food blogs, postfeminism, and the communication of expertise.* Lexington.

Projansky, S. (2014). *Spectacular girls: Media fascination and celebrity culture.* New York University Press.

Rodney, A., Cappeliez, S., Oleschuk, M., & Johnston, J. (2017). The online domestic goddess: An analysis of food blog femininities. *Food, Culture, & Society, 20*(4), 685–707. 10.1080/15528014.2017.1357954

Salvio, P. M. (2012). Dishing it out: Food blogs and post-feminist domesticity. *Gastronomica, 12*(3), 31–39. 10.1525/GFC.2012.12.3.31

Saveur. (2011, May 17). The 2011 SAVEUR best food blog awards: The winners. *Saveur.* https://www.saveur.com/article/Kitchen/2011-SAVEUR-Best-Food-Blog-Awards-Winners/

Saveur. (2019, August 29). Meet the winners of the 2019 SAVEUR blog awards. *Saveur.* https://www.saveur.com/winners-2019-saveur-blog-awards/

Serazio, M. (2013). *Your ad here: The cool sell of guerrilla marketing.* New York University Press.

Shapiro, L. (1986). *Perfection salad: Women and cooking at the turn of the century.* University of California Press.

Siles, I. (2011). From online filter to web format: Articulating materiality and meaning in the early history of blogs. *Social Studies of Science, 41*(5), 737–758. doi:10.1177/0306312711420190

Suthivarakom, G. (2011, May 9). A brief history of food blogs. *Saveur.* https://www.saveur.com/article/Kitchen/A-Brief-Food-Blog-Timeline

Tasker, Y., & Negra, D. (2007). *Interrogating postfeminism: Gender and the politics of popular culture.* Duke University Press.

Tran, T. (2020). Imagining the perfect Asian woman through hate: Michelle Phan, anti-Phandom, and Asian diasporic beauty cultures. *Communication, Culture & Critique. 13*(3), 349–366. 10.93/ccc/tcz057

Tye, D. (2010). *Baking as biography: A life in recipes.* McGill-Queens University Press.

Vavrus, M. D. (2012). Postfeminist redux? *The Review of Communication, 12*(3), 224–236. 10.1080/15358593.2012.671350

Walker Rettberg, J. (2014). *Blogging.* Polity.

Wilson, J., & Yochim, E. C. (2017). *Mothering through precarity: Women's work and digital media.* Duke University Press.
Yano, C. R. (2013). *Pink globalization: Hello Kitty's trek across the Pacific.* Duke University Press.
Zhao, S., Grasmuck, S., & Martin, J. (2008). Identity construction on Facebook: Digital empowerment in anchored relationships. *Computers in Human Behavior, 24*(5), 1816–1836. 10.1016/j.chb.2008.02.012

2 Asian-Inspired: Branding Race in the Food Blogosphere

> - you look weird.
> that's not a question.
> - i meant, what is your ancestry?
> my pops is chinese and my mum is new york (but before that, hungarian)! i'm chinese and jewish, i celebrate christmas, hanukkah, and three new years, and i like pastrami in my egg rolls!
> —Molly Yeh, n.d., *My Name is Yeh*

Molly Yeh is a successful food blogger who was the winner of Saveur's prestigious Blog of the Year award in 2015 and has hosted her own Food Network television show, *Girl Meets Farm*, since 2018. The above excerpt is taken from her blog's About page, on which she publishes answers to frequently asked questions. Its appearance on this page indicates the common practice of asking bloggers of color to identify their racial and ethnic heritage, a microaggresion that affirms the normative whiteness of the blogosphere. Yeh draws attention to this subtext, using the phrasing 'you look weird' to provide a gentle rebuke of this line of questioning, forcing the imagined reader to pause and reflect on the assumptions contained therein. Yet, ultimately, Yeh adheres to the resolutely positive tone that is cultivated in the food blogosphere: her list of 'three new years,' Christmas and Hanukkah alludes to the riches and abundance of a celebrated multiculturalism; the reference to pastrami egg rolls evokes the curiosity and creative possibilities of cultural fusion. Her excitement manifests through the multiple exclamation marks that punctuate these sentences. This positive, postrace expression of race

DOI: 10.4324/9781003302278-2

is also what allows Yeh to strategically deploy her own heritage in the service of authority and authenticity as a blogger, publishing a number of Jewish and Chinese recipes on her blog and in media outlets, and demonstrating how non-whiteness can be a valuable marker of difference to carve out a niche brand in an increasingly overcrowded food blogosphere.

In this chapter, I perform a close analysis of three blogs – *Constellation Inspiration*, *Chinese Grandma*, and *Just Hungry* – to explore the different ways that race is incorporated into the performance of self which is central to food blogs. While this analysis demonstrates the unique and diverse strategies for expressing race as part of digital identity, these strategies are limited through overarching affordances which yield common understandings of race as a commodity that has exchange value, as a marker of positive difference, and as a trait that freely circulates and can be transcended or adopted by choice. I contextualize these findings within the cultural appropriation articulated in hooks' (1992) original formulation of eating the Other while interrogating how the logics of self-branding complicate these arguments. I note that the politics of eating the Other become less clear when individual Asian American bloggers adopt such practices not simply as profit-generating activities but as anchored digital identity performances.

Recipes as Autobiographical Life Writing

Cooking literature have undertaken many different forms in Western history including handwritten aides-memoires scrawled in domestic manuals; home collections of clippings, marginalia and recipe cards; collectively compiled community and church cookbooks; and, more recent celebrity-chef offerings replete with autobiographical narratives and glossy, glamorously styled images. These texts, and the ways that food and food writing reflect power relations, particularly around gender, class and race, have provided the source of inspiration for many scholars who argue for the everyday politics inherent to food literature. Feminist food scholars and historians have turned to food writing and particularly cookbooks as an important and rare site for centering women's voices and recording women's everyday experiences. Within most scholarship on food writing, feminocentricity is presumed. Historians are in consensus that the majority of authors and readers of cookbooks were women (Appadurai, 1988; Neuhaus, 1999; McFeely, 2001; Theophano, 2002; Inness, 2006) and that, through their focus on the female subject, food writing uniquely records women's autobiographies by providing intimate snapshots of women's daily lives (Neuhaus, 1999; Theophano, 2002; Tye, 2010; Avakian, 2014). A further feminist argument for the everyday subversion of food writing arises through the notions of exchange that are inherent to recipes (Leonardi, 1989), which have provided the grounds for collective consciousness amongst women (Inness, 2006; Tye, 2010).

Contained within these arguments – which, in general, enthusiastically recount the feminist potential of these texts and their subjects – is an inevitable acceptance of the limits to these feminist politics. For instance, the feminist potential of cooking literature argued above does not challenge the notion that cookbooks have conflated food work with 'natural' femininity and an idealized gendered identity – which can be seen in cookbooks' historical role as objects that marked a woman's coming of age through marriage and the formal responsibility for a household's cooking and domestic labor (Theophano, 2002) and cookbooks' inverse suggestion that men are unwilling and unable to cook, aside from the occasional, hypermasculinized act of barbequing (DeVault, 1994; Neuhaus, 1999). This binary gendered difference holds even through popular 'exceptions' to the domestic cookbook such as Peg Bracken's 1960 *I Hate to Cook Book* and Poppy Cannon's 1967 *The Can-Opener Cook Book*, both of which acknowledged women's responsibilities in the kitchen even as they sought to mildly protest such obligations. Additionally, while Inness (2006) argues that cookbooks offered women and minority groups the potential to author and circulate political tracts, ultimately she acknowledges the reality that they rarely did so. Moreover, in the postfeminist era, the normativity of women's food work is justified through its reconceptualization as creative self-actualization and self-care, no longer practiced as a gendered obligation but as an empowering and pleasurable choice (e.g. Avakian, 2014; Counihan, 2018; McFeely, 2001; Tye, 2010). It is important to note that encoded in these studies of the feminist potential of food writing is a disproportionate focus on the contexts and experiences of privileged white domestic food workers.

These cookbook analyses and their varied interpretations underline the importance of contextualizing food work and writing, which has also been a feature of the analysis of immigrant food writing. Cookbooks have been explored as valuable sites for invoking the communities, traditions, and embodied practices that contribute to identity formation for immigrant and diasporic communities. Cookbooks often trace the transnational flows of imagined communities of women and the food objects and practices that travel with them, offering an understanding of the immigrant and diasporic experience that organically speaks to the complexities of this subject positioning. They encompass historical and community practices that tie immigrants to an imagined homeland and record the various ways in which different food histories, rituals and practices are fused, substituted, and translated – a culinary metaphor for how immigrant peoples are integrated, assimilated and alienated within dominant Western cultures (Inness, 2001; Mannur, 2013; Epp, 2015).

At the same time, 'ethnic' food media is readily used as a form of soft diplomacy that obfuscates the lived experiences and realities of cultural assimilation, discrimination and alienation by diasporic communities. Several scholars have noted how immigrant or ethnic cookbooks have been used to variously promote multiculturalism and assimilation by presenting ethnic foods as enticing fare for an assumed white audience (Negra, 2002; Bell & Hollows, 2007). In such media, immigrant foods and cultures are typically described as 'easy' and 'fun' (rhetoric which continues to be widely used in the contemporary food blogosphere) which is assumed to similarly be applicable to the process of cultural integration and fusion. However, this use of ethnic food and foodways as a palatable metaphor for acceptance of the Other is often effortlessly transformed into a project of cultural appropriation and imperialism, coupling this conditional acceptance to readily shifting hierarchies of taste for ethnic and exoticized foods that are variously rejected and incorporated into a dominant white culture by the whims of hegemonic structural forces.

Identity performance is central to the food blogosphere and the success of food blogs as brands ties into this longer history of autobiographical life writing through food literature. Indeed, it is truistic to argue that food blogs are autobiographical, as personalized life narratives are characteristic of the genre and made far more explicit than in the recipe cards and community cookbooks that were the objects of focus in the studies referenced above. Additionally, while the narratives published in the food blogosphere are ostensibly about food, food bloggers contextualize recipes through details of traditions, family memories, and geographical landscapes that give rise to the possibility for valuable personalized expressions of the Asian diasporic and Asian American experiences. In this manner, food blogs depart from the ethos of immigrant cookbooks in which "many authors militantly defended the cooking of their own community ... rejoiced in their own culinary heritage and "publicized" it" (LeDantec-Lowry, 2008, p. 114) and instead allow for more nuanced and intimate reflections on the everyday processes by which individual women in the Asian diaspora and Asian American communities undertake the journey of 'making sense' of their racial identities within their specific familial, geographical and cultural environments. That is, while none of the bloggers examined here explicitly propose or articulate a desire to explore Asian American identity through their blogs, such explorations routinely surface organically through the conventions of the genre which value expressions of race as markers of authenticity and niche branding, and compel the inclusion of personal narratives for contextualizing recipes. These individual stories situate immigrant foods and the lived experience of postrace subjectivity in ways that do not necessarily elide processes of appropriation and authority but demonstrate how such processes are enacted as negotiations by individuals within their quotidian routines. These negotiations of raced identity performance are made salient through consideration of platform affordances and commercial conventions of the genre.

Containing Race in the Database

The performance of race in the food blogosphere is facilitated through the structure of the digital form, a feature of which is the interplay of database and narrative which yields particular ways of potentially including and excluding racial identities. The database is described by Lev Manovich as the "structured collection of data ... organized for fast search and retrieval by a computer" (2000, p. 194). Manovich theorizes the database in binary opposition to narrative form, contrasting digital database organization with novels and films to argue that

> new media objects do not tell stories; they don't have beginning or end; in fact, they don't have any development, thematically, formally or otherwise which would organize their elements into a sequence. Instead, they are collections of individual items, where every item has the same significance as any other.
>
> (Manovich, 2000)

However, this binary characterization of the database has since been critiqued by many scholars, particularly in the digital humanities. Notably, Kate Hayles (2007) has argued for an understanding of database and narrative as 'natural symbionts,' noting that databases generate relational meaning between elements, while Marsha Kinder explores the potential of *database narratives* where "story possibilities seem limitless, where randomness, repetition, and interruptions are rampant, and where search engines are motored by desire" (2002, p. 8).

Food blogs offer a way of further thinking through the potential of *database narratives* which are modularized and structured within the database, but also tell and retell narratives that are nonlinear and dialogic.

Database logics are made most prominent on food blogs through the menu structure. Menus have a dual meaning in English, used both to connote the list of items available for sale in a restaurant as well as the list of commands displayed on screen in computing. The former provides a representation of meals as consumable commodities, arranging them in a sequential fashion (Appadurai, 1988). The latter works as a directive, interfacing the desires of the computer user with a store of organized commands. The menu systems that structure food blogs draw on both of these qualities to arrange bloggers' content. Food blogs typically include elaborate, overlapping menu systems which variously give an overview of the blog's purpose as well as organizing and hierarchizing the abundance of published content. For instance, menus categorize recipes in different ways that align with individual food blog brands (e.g. spring, summer, fall, winter or fruit, meat, sweets, vegetable). Menus also create space for paratextual information that works alongside the recipes and narrative content that constitutes the main body of text on the blog. This paratextual content includes the 'About' page as well as tabs variously titled 'Contact', 'Press' or 'Work With Me' which allude to the discrete categorization of audiences as readers or commercial partners.

Menus and the database are inherently ambiguous; they demonstrate the potential to variously create exclusionary divides as well as to generate productive new associations. On one hand, menus and their work of containing and excluding can be used to assert dominance. Appadurai has explained the colonizing force of menus in contemporary Indian cookbooks, noting that

> while, in European and some other cuisines, the idea of a food menu is associated with a succession of courses, Indian meals do not normally have a significant sequential dimension. Everything arrives more or less at once in most everyday contexts, although certain key liquid accompaniments to the base grains and certain key condiments may appear at different points.
>
> (1988, p. 20)

The outcome of such cookbook menus is to subordinate regional and local cuisines beneath an overarching, hegemonic Indian national cuisine (Appadurai, 1988). This characterization of menus as fixing order and asserting hierarchies through binary logics demonstrate an enactment of discrete and impermeable categorization.

On the other hand, the digital menu system facilitates the searchability and indexing of content, promoting the operation of the food blogosphere as a gift economy for food pedagogies. Menus archive and index information on food work, making content easily searchable and accessible. Additionally, the menu's archival function generates visibility and value for typically ephemeral reproductive labor, supporting a feminist transformation of the temporality and banality of "day-to-day maintenance: feeding and cleaning and mending and feeding and cleaning ... distinctly monotonous and in a tangible sense unproductive" (Shapiro, 1986, p. 13). The way that menus capture such domestic outputs – even though they are stylized renditions of reproductive labor – ascribes value to domestic food work and builds sizeable archives that, over time, help to capture the scope and scale of women's work. Moreover, in addition to normalizing mundane expression through the regular updating of content, food blogs naturally interweave posts that track the feminine lifecycle over time as bloggers include posts celebrating traditional feminized milestones such as engagements, weddings, pregnancies and moving house, as well as annual holidays and seasonal events. The menu structure enables the coexistence of these relatively fluid and oppositional temporalities, parsing autobiographical narratives into modular units that generate non-linear and non-chronological temporalities that challenge both the compulsory feminine milestones of postfeminist subjectivity (Negra, 2009) as well as the cyclical time that entraps women in and through reproductive labor (Kristeva, 1981).

The role of the database in structuring postfeminist Asian American subjectivity, and the productivity of the menu's ambiguity for negotiating a hybrid Chinese Canadian diasporic identity, can be explored through *Constellation Inspiration*, a baking and desserts blog authored by blogger Amy Ho. On this blog, race is made visible through the main menu which features the categories: 'cake', 'cookies,' 'cream puffs,' 'tarts,' 'bars,' 'candy,' 'Asian-inspired' and 'seasonal.' While the first six categories reflect *Constellation Inspiration's* overarching focus on baking by dividing sweets into intricate subcategories, and the 'seasonal' tab alludes to the importance of holidays such as Christmas and Valentine's Day in inspiring content across the blogosphere, the 'Asian-inspired' tab marks a categorical separation which at once makes race prominently visible on the front page of the blog, while also cleanly demarcating these 'foreign' ingredients and desserts from the remaining, conventionally Western, baking categories. This menu positioning reinforces the dominant normativity of Western baking traditions on this food blog and the assumed inability to assimilate Asian tastes within this foodscape. Moreover, Ho reproduces a binary relationship of inferiority as she introduces the recipes in her 'Asian-inspired' category as both mundane and inferior – "not as 'fancy' [as the] things you would see at fancy bakeshops and patisseries" (Ho, n.d.b.) – and as specialties that she has long ignored over the course of her impressive self-taught baking career. In this binary framing of Asian and Western desserts, Ho demonstrates a simultaneous distancing and embrace of Asian identity, which is common among diasporic voices (Ma, 1998).

The menu structure of Ho's narrative facilitates the expression of her Chinese Canadian diasporic identity as a journey made up of a continuous series of negotiations that are mapped onto the affective memories conjured up by certain foods and experiences rather than through the strict chronology of linear autobiographies. The affective resonance of diasporic identity is narrated through the blog's overarching themes and aesthetics of a girlish childhood. The About section uses poetic, embellished language to describe the blog as a series of love letters, both to sweets and to the reader, and is used to symbolize Ho's love affair with baking, simultaneously capturing the girlish themes of romance, sweetness, and journal-writing (Ho, n.d. a.). While, as is conventional in most food blogs, Ho's face and body are not prominently featured in the food images on the blog (Dejmanee, 2016) she frequently uses photos that include her hands within the frame, emphasizing the 'handcrafted' work of her stylized recipes and photography while de-emphasizing the embodied labor of her hands as they are captured in still image and reveal nails painted with glittery accents and pastel colors, suggesting their role as accessories in the image rather than their work in production. Furthermore, a particularly postfeminist investment in 'girlie culture' (Baumgardner & Richards, 2010) is evidenced through an exaggerated femininity and cuteness, referenced through rendering things miniature, such as the intricate gingerbread greenhouse she adorns with small snow-covered trees and tiny fairy lights; drawing on icons of cute culture, such as the Japanese cartoon creature Totoro, in her food designs; relishing "any opportunity to turn scary Halloween characters into something cuter and more approachable" (Ho, 2020); and, styling her baked goods with flowers, sprinkles, and gold leaf accents.

Such girlish and cute food work ties into broader food trends – notably, the ubiquity of rainbow-hued unicorn food and funfetti, as well as the popularity of intricate, miniature sweets such as cake pops, cupcakes and macarons. However, this girlishness situates Ho within a perpetual childhood which minimizes Ho's success as a cookbook author and food blogger, but also allows her to explore the melancholy of the Asian diasporic experience. For instance, Ho connects many of her 'Asian-inspired' recipes to childhood experiences that describe a sense of loss. She writes of the ubiquity of Chinese desserts and recipes which she regards as cheap and ever-present in her childhood, and which has long led her to reject learning how to make these items herself. However, she notes that her interest in learning how to make Chinese desserts is piqued as she yearns for the Chinese bakeries that are becoming less accessible as she gets older. As she writes in her post titled 'Grilled Chewy Rice Cake,'

> I've never thought of making these rice cakes because they're usually $1 at the bakery; I didn't see the need or have the desire to make them because they're so affordable to buy. Now that I see these rice cakes less and less, I needed my own recipe as a backup.
> (Ho, 2021)

Similarly, she writes that she finally begins to take an interest in re-creating the Chinese desserts usually prepared by her mother and eaten at her parents' house once she realizes that she will not be able to rely on her mother to make them forever. These narratives frame Ho's understanding of her Chinese diasporic identity as a loss, alluding to the ways that immigrant relations have often been figured from the perspective of the dominant country, for instance, through loss of jobs and wages which are threatened by arriving immigrants, through the loss of cultural homogeneity, typically framed through fear and threat (Ma, 1998). However, Ho's narrative documents the kinds of loss that are experienced by diasporic subjects themselves, entailing the loss of context and traditions that bind one to unknown ancestors and compel a personal responsibility to reclaim and revive such knowledges against a host of barriers.

This framing of racial identity as loss allows Ho to draw on the postfeminist makeover narrative to use this as the grounds for embarking on an understanding and reconstruction of her Chinese diasporic identity as a personal journey. That is, as Ho documents the journey of teaching herself the techniques for baking and mastering Asian desserts, in the same fashion that she records the process of learning how to create choux pastry and financiers, she materializes her racial identity as a creative, learned process, expressed through the metaphor of recreating the foods that tangibly connect her to Chinese tastes and traditions. This creative process is indicated through the use of the word 'inspired' which is hyphenated to Asian, a hyphen which acknowledges both the exploration of pan-Asian flavors, techniques and recipes as well as Ho's assertion of creative license to interpret the Asian recipes of her childhood in a non-traditional way. This results in artistic renditions of moon cakes with sago pearls that are decorated with vivid purple and pink swirls; and flecked with gold leaf; heart-shaped taro balls in her sago dessert soup; and hybrid cultural concoctions such as matcha neopolitan sugar cookies and Chinese 'white rabbit candy' cupcakes. Moreover, this framing of race as a personal journey means that Ho's position as an authority to speak about Chinese traditions at times wavers – her confident use of Chinese characters and translations is paired with external references to Wikipedia or news articles to explain the meanings of Chinese New Year and Togetherness Cookie Boxes. This is an indication of the kinds of knowledge that are translated through the Asian diaspora – knowledges that are sometimes partial and fragmentary, sometimes encoded with an uncertainty as to whether they are inspired more by one's own familial variations on the culture, and divorced from a contextual or in-depth historical knowledge of these traditions and celebrations but remembered through the embodied practices and domestic rituals, as well as evocatively through the tastes and textures of food objects. The menu structure documents these creative experiments to learn about and master Asian desserts in a way that maps the meaning and relevance of diasporic hybridity within Ho's daily lived experience.

Through this example, it is possible to see how blog menus offer multiple ways to ambiguously and productively express racial identity within the dominant frameworks of postfeminist and postrace discourse. In this case, Ho's narration of her Chinese diasporic experience benefits from the temporal simultaneity facilitated by the database, for while the lens of childhood typically encodes in it a sense of transience, Ho's blog is able to remain fixed on a stylized girlishness in which she grapples with her relationship to Asia, particularly as this connotes her evolving relationship with her parents and is marked through the foods and celebrations that most evocatively make this relationship material in her daily life. The database narrative allows for certain meaningful experiences and evocative objects to be emphasized, and for Ho to ruminate on the significance of select childhood events while also documenting how her understanding of her own Chinese Canadian identity changes over time. Indeed, Ho spends time recreating and adapting recipes that she has previously posted, presenting a diasporic autobiographical narrative that is aligned to the memories and affective responses that organically arise in the course of everyday routines rather than linear time. The menu structure supports an understanding of diasporic identity as a partial and dynamic process – a shifting and fragmentary collection of memories and encounters that are constantly being re-negotiated. While I have noted that Ho's framing of racial identity as a personal journey approximates the postfeminist makeover project, the database elides the easy distinction of 'before' and 'after,' and does not allow for a final makeover 'moment' or big reveal but, rather, is comprised of many small moments of shifting perspective. It is such partial and fragmentary explorations that demonstrate Asian American food bloggers' potential engagement with hybridity – as an expression of the porousness and situatedness of identity (Ang, 2001) – as a political act.

Hybridity is effectively captured by the organizational structures of the database. After all, for all their attempts to contain and organize, scaffold and separate, menu categories are inherently leaky and objects constantly blur category boundaries: Tanghulu-style strawberries must be doubly categorised under both 'Asian-inspired' and 'candy'; the 'Matcha Mascarpone Cream Tartlets' which do not appear under the 'Asian-inspired' tag are prefaced by reference to the fruit custard tarts that Ho describes as a staple after-school snack from the Chinese bakery. Furthermore, while I have argued that on the surface the 'Asian-inspired' tab appears to exclude, separating Ho's Asian treats from those emanating from Western baking traditions, from the perspective of the Asian diasporic reader, it might also be understood as inclusive, highlighting the collection of recipes and memories that are most likely to be meaningful within this community and, in doing so, acknowledging this often invisible audience and centering their experiences. It is this ambiguity of the menu that is inherently productive in the exploration of the Asian American food blogger's diasporic experience.

Self-Branding and Race as Lifestyle Philosophy

In a digital environment in which creative choices are inextricable from commercial logics, another plausible reason as to why 'Asian-inspired' content assumes such prominence on *Constellation Inspiration* is due to the fact that these recipes attract significant search engine hits for the site. In the food blogosphere, even where Asian identity is presented as an intimate and reflective personal journey, these expressions necessarily emerge through the overarching logics of self-branding. Alison Hearn describes self-branding as a rhetorical strategy that involves "creating a detachable, saleable image or narrative, which effectively circulates cultural meanings" (2008, p. 198) and a form of labor that is designed to "produce cultural value and, potentially, material profit" (2008, p. 198). Sarah Banet-Weiser further argues that self-branding strategies, postfeminist subjectivity and the interactive affordances of digital technologies cohere to produce a moral framework that "make[s] self-branding seem not only logical but perhaps necessary" (2012, p. 56) as a way of demonstrating the capacity and empowerment of the postfeminist subject through their digital identity construction. The labor of self-branding becomes visible on food blogs in the ways that personal narratives and identity performances are tied together under an overarching ethos that situates each food blog within a uniquely identified niche, aimed at maximizing the blog's compatibility with consumer demographics, and encouraging coherence across blogging content. The collapse of food blogs, brands and individual identities is made evident through the use of the blog name as the domain name, the header which navigates the reader back to the 'home' page of the blog site, and the name with which bloggers identify in the online space. Bloggers often articulate 'tag lines' which make clear the ethos of their blogs, for instance to showcase 'easy comfort food' or 'seasonal inspirational meal ideas,' and produce content and images that consistently demonstrates adherence to these representational goals.

One of the impacts of self-branding is its tendency to modularize identity, emphasizing those aspects that can be readily valued in commercial culture. Race typically presents an ideal identity characteristic for non-white subjects to showcase a kind of difference that can readily be used to distinguish blogger's brands and, when presented as a commodity, is currently highly valued for its association with exoticism and adventurousness in contemporary foodie culture (Johnston & Baumann, 2010). In fact, Asian American food bloggers are often compelled to reference their non-whiteness, and to incorporate it meaningfully into the ethos of their food blog and identity performance. For example, on the blog *Chinese Grandma,* the compulsion to make race visible and legible within the logics of self-branding and postrace discourse results in the presentation of race as a mutable property, articulated as a lifestyle philosophy and set of positive, personal characteristics. This is detailed in a bookmarked post in which blogger Lillian pays homage to her two biological grandmothers whom she refers to as 'the real Chinese grandmas,' described as 'survivors' who "lived lives of courage, strength and tenacity" (2010) in overcoming war, poverty and hardship to raise and provide for their families. This story is supported through very brief biographical highlights of their lives, including their journeys from China to Korea and then, for her maternal grandmother, realizing her dream of moving to the United States. The post continues with a paragraph describing her mother's life and tracing how the qualities of strength and joy are sustained through the maternal line, before concluding the post by referencing her circle of friends. She writes:

> Chinese and not, we come from the tradition of practicality, frugality, resourcefulness, hard work. We are achievement-oriented but love to save our paychecks for the freedom and security that comes from money in the bank. We spend on what's important to us, and we are sticklers for quality. We are curious about the world and love travel. We love home cooking from all cultures. We have an expansive definition of family (my kids have more aunties than they can keep track of). We share truth – the good, the bad, the boring. We are together for the long haul.
> (Lillian, 2010)

This lineage that Lillian traces, from her biological grandmothers, to her mother, and then to her close friends yields a definition of family that is both constructed and biological, and a way of reckoning with the distant admiration and loss that permeates Lillian's relationship to her biological grandmothers, who passed away when she was young and with whom she was never able to fluently communicate (2010). In the face of these barriers to connecting with her ancestors, Lillian makes sense of the fact that she does not share the economic, cultural or linguistic environments of her forebears through a focus on the shared personal characteristics she imagines does bond them, notably thrift, resourcefulness and caring. However, this also leads to a very generalizable, postrace understanding of race as a set of personal characteristics that can be – and, according to Lillian, *are* – adopted by people of any racial or ethnic background. That is, race is transformed into a set of qualities that can be adapted by anyone which has the effect of reductively transforming Chinese identity to this set of legible and positive characteristics that can be adopted by choice. In this sense, even though Lillian's Chinese ancestry is highlighted through the brand name and her blogger pseudonym throughout the site, race becomes just another label for describing identity on her site, one which is uncomplicated and just as influential as her identification as a native Californian who "geeks out over fresh fruits and vegetables, farmers markets and artisan food makers" (Lillian, n.d.). In this way, race is realized as a commodity that is fluid, transferable, and consumable for privileged postrace subjects who are able to 'transcend' markers of race.

Through this commoditization of her Chinese identity, Lillian foregrounds the flexibility of race as a disembodied brand strategy. Thrift becomes part of her online persona and digital brand. Lillian's resourcefulness is indicated through multiple recipes for muffins and breads that use up browned bananas, and a post in which Lillian goes through her detailed hacks to optimize peanut butter and jelly sandwiches by reducing the sogginess of the bread and minimizing food wastage. Lillian showcases her renovated kitchen which has been painstakingly designed to increase its efficiency, and marvels at the domestic tips and tricks brought into her house by a steady stream of close friends. This flexible interpretation and performance of what it means to be Chinese allows for an endless fluidity. Lillian often provides dual interpretations of Chinese dishes that come from her mother, detailing both her mother's preferences and her own adaptations to recipes (e.g. meatballs that are baked versus fried; beans that are sliced straight or diagonally; won tons that are folded flat or standing up) in a way that celebrates the personalization and shifts that take place to recipes over time. This maps onto racial heritage onto the malleability of recipes – and the endless ways they are exchanged and adapted – promoting the idea of a harmonious, postrace multiculturalism within which Lillian's collection of 'great easy Asian recipes' can be readily enjoyed.

In postrace literature, scholars have convincingly pointed out the ways in which such a generalizable, commoditized understanding of race actively erases its embodied and historical significance, suggesting a casual egalitarianism to race as something that can be adopted by choice or transcended by omission. Such processes of commoditization, bell hooks (1992) argues, are the foundations for the appropriation, colonization, and fetishization of racial stereotypes. However, Lillian's work – as that of other Asian American food bloggers – also resists such easy analysis. Lillian's work challenges the representational stereotypes of Chinese women which, in mainstream Western media, have overwhelmingly made race hypervisible through offensive caricatures and exaggerated negative perceptions. In response, Lillian's blog situates Chinese heritage within the everyday and the domestic – her allusions to race are nestled within a plethora of written reflections on life, including grappling with identity shifts of motherhood and the chaos of moving house with four young children. The significance of race in her daily life shines through in glimpses of the wonton folding techniques her mother is teaching her kindergartner, and in the soy marinade she prepares for her Costco fish fillets which allude to longer histories and contexts for her racial identity. Moreover, the blog narrative format allows her space to articulate her own understandings of the nuances of Chinese American culture. For example, she discusses the recipe for Chinese-American General Tso's chicken produced in the *Lucky Peach* cookbook by Peter Meehan and Momofuku's David Chang and while she celebrates the cookbook's self-claim of being '100% inauthentic' and adaptations of Asian recipes for home cooks, she also admits that the cookbook's intentionally campy design and photography "makes me laugh, but ruefully – to non-Asians it's a wry joke, but if you're really Asian, part of you is genuinely cringing" (Lillian, 2016). Similarly, she publishes a long bullet-point essay in response to tiger mom Amy Chua, with her response organized under the subheadings 'positive,' 'outdated,' and 'dangerous' ideas. In this essay Lillian notes the complexities for Chinese Americans who may recognize these parenting stereotypes while pushing back against their limitations, but ultimately ending with the universalizing experience of parenting and noting that "Chua was brave to present such a detestable portrait of herself as a lesson for others [as] many of us don't want to admit that sometimes we are not our best selves as parents" (Lillian, 2010). These nuanced reflections on the complexities of the everyday experiences of race are positioned alongside the commoditization of race and the explicit appeals to its coherent and commercially viable operation as a brand strategy.

In reference to eating the Other, the value of Asian food blogs certainly seems to eagerly participate in 'spicing up' the bland hegemony of white culture, a process which hooks (1992) argues serves to affirm white supremacist capitalist patriarchy. It is clear that there are elements of this use of race as a postrace strategy to indicate a valued 'difference' in the commercialized food blogosphere. It is through these logics that Chinese becomes a lifestyle philosophy practiced by choice. At the same time, there are clearly qualitative differences between the kinds of stylized identity performance engaged by bloggers, and the commercial appropriation of culture in popular culture that hooks critiques. One of the main differences is where hooks argues that racial appropriation flourishes through the systematic de-contextualization and de-historicization of cultural objects, in the case of food blogs, food and food pedagogies are relentlessly contextualized within the personal histories and individual experiences of the blogger. This centers the narratives and experiences of Asian diasporic identities, allowing them to assert creative agency over their work and to use their accompanying written reflections to highlight their unique and authoritative voices over their experiences and foodscapes. And, while the possibilities indicated by these conventions are in some ways applicable across the blogosphere, the examples by Asian American bloggers reveal ways in which voice is used to 'speak back' to expectations, stereotypes and erasures of the Asian diasporic experience.

Authenticity and Cultural Translation

The success of self-branding in the food blogosphere is often contingent upon the performance of authenticity, which is linked to the realization of the commercial value upon which self-branding strategies are oriented. As Banet-Weiser argues, "self-branding is an expression of a moral framework, a means to access 'authenticity,' and crucially important in order to become 'more of who you are' as well as who 'you were meant to be'" (2012, p. 59). In this understanding, self-branding and authenticity are about cultivating cultural and affective relationships, which are essential to the logics of food blogs. Authenticity in the food blogosphere is often performed through sharing personal experiences and mundane details of intimate life in a manner reminiscent of 'relational labor,' described by Nancy Baym, as the "regular, ongoing communication with audiences over time to build social relationships that foster paid work" (2015, p. 16). Relational labor tends to highlight the inextricable ways in which authenticity, as part of online identity performance, can never be separated from the profit-accumulating logics of self-branding strategy. That is, while authenticity never exists as a 'pure' space or connotes a 'real' online self, it is capable of generating real affective relationships, which may be oriented towards producing value for the blogger. However, for Asian American bloggers, in addition to sharing mundane details about their lives, racial authenticity is typically demonstrated by highlighting their authority to *translate*, making clear the assumption of a hegemonic, white audience for their work

The value ascribed to the Asian American food blogger as translator is partly driven by contemporary foodie culture which, like the food blogosphere, has been catalogued as "normatively white and affluent" (Johnston & Baumann, 2010, p. 16) and driven by the overarching ethos of cultural omnivorousness – in which the elite, snobbish connotations of the 'foodie' are replaced by an engaged adventurousness and curiosity towards food. Yet, in replacing expensive 'fine dining' with omnivorous eating that challenges previous markers of high/low culture, food is now subject to distinction through hierarchical markers such as "quality, rarity, locality, organic, hand-made, creativity, and simplicity" (Johnston & Baumann, 2010, p. 3). Within this new cultural canon, foods are highly valued for their exoticism and cosmopolitanism, as well as for their perceived authenticity, opening up a valuable market for Asian American food bloggers to serve as cultural intermediaries who can both make claims to the authenticity of their 'exotic' recipes while simultaneously translating them in a way that is legible for the eager foodie outsider. It is just such a project that serves as the explicit goal of Makiko Itoh's blog, *Just Hungry*. Itoh explicitly states that her blog aims to meet the needs of English-speaking readers who wish to cook Japanese food but don't speak Japanese, going so far as to reject the possibility of including Japanese translations of her recipes (even though she has worked as a translator of cookbooks from Japanese to English) as she explains that translations would detract from the intended purpose of her blog project (Itoh, 2010). Given this stated aim, Itoh is required to both demonstrate her claims of 'authentic' knowledge of Japanese food and culture as well as her competency as a translator for her non-Japanese audience.

The word 'authentic' is used multiple times throughout *Just Hungry* with the performance of this knowledge expressed through Itoh relaying her experiences of her family, her childhood and mundane experiences that are set in or reference Japan, such as watching a Japanese cooking show on TV as inspiration for a summer peach pasta recipe; her mum's tradition of pickling umeboshi plums each year; and, a lifechanging food memoir by Katsura Morimura which she finds in the school library of an elementary school in Hachioji. These intimate experiences of Japanese culture approximate authenticity through their qualities of being mundane and embodied, and the specificity with which they are recounted. Itoh supplements such experiences with her authoritative knowledge of Japanese food through the inclusion of many details that suggest an encyclopedic knowledge of Japanese foods, histories and traditions. Itoh is a professional writer, and her blog reflects this for while her food photography and website design are quite simple, her writing is full of richness and detail that clearly show off her knowledge of historical events in Japanese culture as well as food traditions, supplementing the knowledge of Japanese food culture that comes from her matrilineal traditions.

In addition to her appeals to authenticity, Itoh assures readers of her competency to translate Japanese recipes for English-speaking audience, noting her fluency in English and her experiences living in several Western countries including in the US and the UK. Itoh further situates Japanese food within a global landscape and her cosmopolitan identity, describing in detail her experiences and frustrations with trying to recreate authentic Japanese dishes in the US and Europe. Itoh includes a series of food translation guides on her blog, including 'The essential staples of a Japanese pantry,' (Itoh, 2006) 'Japanese grocery store list' (Itoh, 2008c) and 'The Japanese food and cooking lexicon' (Itoh, 2008a). This work is enshrined on her blog through attention to the pantry staples required in a basic Japanese kitchen, with detailed notes on acceptable brands, suggested price points, and online suppliers. She also provides long responses in the comments sections of her recipes, which respond to further questions on substitutions and techniques. However, throughout this project Itoh simultaneously reveals the inherent tenuousness of cultural authenticity. Itoh painstakingly outlines acceptable substitutions and variations that remain true to the spirit of Japanese food, yet qualifies her authority by explaining that her knowledge of Japanese food does not extend to regional variations or to specific dishes produced by Japanese restaurants across the world. She traces the detailed histories and origins of Japanese foods and traditions as a paean to authenticity. Yet, throughout this project, Itoh is required to grapple with the tension inherent to her quest to preserve and document authenticity, an impossible project in a landscape where culture – and the identity performance she constructs within it – is subject to a continuous process of reconstruction and renegotiation.

That is, while Itoh's dedication to food research and knowledge is unassailable, Itoh includes as the fourth question on her FAQ page, "Are you really Japanese? I read somewhere that you're not Japanese, or you're half/hapa, or from Hawaii" (Itoh, 2010), This question, and Itoh's editorial decision to include it on her blog, raises several interesting points. As with the excerpt from Molly Yeh which opened this chapter, the question highlights the marked-ness of race for non-white bloggers, and heritage for bloggers like Itoh who build their brand so consciously upon the premise of cultural purity. Moreover, as with the phrasing Yeh selected for this inquiry into racial heritage, Itoh's choice of paraphrasing for this question is telling, deviating from the more benign 'What is your background/race?' to a question that amounts to a direct challenge to her identity performance and, along with it, Itoh's authority as a blogger of Japanese food. Ultimately, this obnoxiously-phrased question yields the curt and exasperated response that: "Both my parents are Japanese and so are their ancestors stretching back for many generations as far as we know, and I was born in Tokyo, so I think that makes me 100% Japanese" (Itoh, 2010). While the foodie quest for exoticism and authenticity has previously been critiqued by David Bell and Joanne Hollows as immobilizing the Other in time and space in order to preserve and celebrate "domestic and local culinary practices ... [as] a site of tradition and authenticity in a globalized world" (2007, p. 23), Itoh's work also resists such a reading by demonstrating how deeply her life as a Japanese woman is contextualized within a complex cosmopolitanism and shifting cross-cultural environments. That is, while the presentation of self as a bearer of authentic domestic and cultural knowledge is willingly adopted, and the commoditization of race is a strategy that is strategically deployed, the Asian American food blogger also resists the easy colonization of her knowledge by the reader. Such a response becomes evident in moments of rupture in which the blogger is able to speak back to, and resist, the easy or offensive stereotyping and passive objectification of Asian identity by imperialist foodie cultures.

Ruptures of Melancholy, Loss and Anger

The case studies analyzed in this chapter demonstrate that while each blogger takes a unique approach to constructing a digital self-brand, their strategies are driven by the same logics, which tends to produce homogenous results. One outcome is that, for Asian diasporic food bloggers, race is always made visible, often as a commoditized and positive marker of difference. While some Asian American bloggers may choose to not speak explicitly about race or actively fold their Asian heritage into their brand, and bloggers differ in their decisions to make traces of race more or less visible, in an environment where stories of heritage, family events, traditions, childhood memories, matrilineage and geography are necessary to framing food, race is always marked. Another outcome is that race is often presented using postrace discourses, for example, as a set of qualities that may be circulated or transcended, as a commodity, and as an unequivocally positive multiculturalism or cosmopolitanism. To be clear, this finding is not intended to suggest that the different identity performances and brand strategies of Asian American food bloggers are regressive or racist but, rather, a logical response to the conditions of digital visibility in the attention economy. These identity performances are a testament to the hold of the digital frameworks and commercial logics which structure digital identity expressions in the blogosphere and have resulted in largely aspirational and faithful reproductions of white middle-class gender and lifestyle norms. This points to the limits of digital media in enacting radical identity politics, a finding which has been replicated in other digital cultures (Dobson, 2015; Pham, 2015).

While these structural limitations are significant, it is important to note that discursive silencing and exclusion has always been practiced in and through food media and technologies. For example, while cookbooks have helped historians uncover details about the underdocumented daily lives of women, Theophano (2002) also acknowledges that early cookbooks are only able to reveal information on the lives of those who were privileged enough to own and produce cookbooks, namely, literate upper-class women who had the means to use valuable bound paper notebooks as personal housekeeping manuals. Raffia Zafar examines Quandra Prettyman's provocative question of why so few Black cooks have produced cookbooks, concluding that "[t]he beginnings of an answer lie in the difficulty of writing a book that engages simultaneously with the shadows of Black slavery, servitude, and oppression, the persistence of stereotypes, and the practicalities of cooking" (1999, pp. 449–450). While cookbooks have not been exclusively published by white, middle-class cooks, the platform has been marked by a relative underrepresentation of minority groups due to differences in literacy and access to publishing houses, as well as cultural differences in the production and circulation of written versus oral food pedagogies (Inness, 2006). Such limitations are similarly found in the inherent exclusions of the food blogging form, where it is important to note that the increasingly professionalized quality and skew towards bloggers who perform an aspirational middle-class lifestyle largely dictates visibility and success in the food blogosphere. These structural limitations on identity expression in the blogosphere do not negate the political potential of the food blogosphere – after all, commercialism is always inherent to identity construction in an advanced capitalist society, and stylized performances of authenticity do not necessarily discount the value of sharing intimate personal expressions of underrepresented Asian American women's experiences. Moreover, it would be unfair and probably unproductive to task Asian American food bloggers with the responsibility for enacting radical identity politics through this genre. Instead, I argue that given this context of partial and stylized identity possibilities, and the ambiguity fostered by the technological form, the significance of rupture as an analytical lens makes itself apparent.

I have argued that identity performance in the food blogosphere is structured by logics which produce predictable patterns of identity performance, which tend to produce certain norms, subjects and discourses. Crucially, for these performances to maintain their visibility in the blogosphere – with its endless churning of content – these performances of hegemonic identity must be continuously reproduced and amplified. The digital identity must be continuously reconstructed through content creation and active presence, which generally works to maintain the veneer of ideal identity performance. This leads to the demand, encoded into the conventions of food blogging, that bloggers regularly produce updates across multiple platforms to maintain the relevance of their blogs, which is synonymous with digital visibility. Within these continual reproductions of idealized postrace, postfeminist subjectivity lie the possibilities for everyday subversion, in which individuals detail the ways that the contradictions, limitations and ambiguities of post- ideologies are encountered in their everyday lives. While these possibilities for subversion of the idealized subject are ever-present, then, they become most visible through moments of rupture in which the contradictions and unsustainability of these dominant subject discourses become apparent. A similar attention to the "rare moment[s] in which the post- ideology is ruptured in popular culture" (2009, p. 246) has been documented by Ralina Joseph in Tyra Banks' response to her tabloid media 'fat' scandal, as she angrily breaks down on her talk show, momentarily eschewing her carefully cultivated performance of postrace, postfeminist celebrity to defiantly 'speak back' to her detractors and demonstrate a political consciousness of the structures of gendered and racial oppression.

Within the food blogosphere, moments of rupture become visible when the veneer of effortless cheer and willing servility performed by the Asian American food blogger is punctured by flashes of anger, exasperation, and frustration, which is seen across Makiko Itoh's work. In response to the endless service often expected of the food blogger, Itoh sets out clear limitations on what she will and will not provide through her blog as she writes "it takes a lot of time for me to write out a recipe that is accurate and replicable, so basically I do not give out recipes via email" (2010) She also curtly remarks on her FAQ page that she will not respond to personal email requests for assistance, as "they only help you, not everyone reading the blog" (2010). To one misguided query posted as a comment on her post for Japanese substitutions she remarks: "I have no idea why people keep thinking this [blog] is a shop!" (2008b) and she uses a similar tone to 'speak back' to the appropriation and misappropriation of Japanese food in a global context. She scoffs at and forcefully rebukes the deceptive advice, which she describes as widely circulated in English-speaking food literature, that Mirin can be substituted by vinegar or that Tamari is a 'more pure' form of soy sauce (Itoh, 2012). In this way, Itoh reveals her exasperation and frustration at the regular microaggressions and demands that she encounters, and momentarily disturbs the expectation that the idealized role of the cultural translator, and in many ways the female food blogger, is to exist in a perpetual state of cheerful service to the reader. These ruptures in identity performance work to reveal the contradictions and tenuousness of postfeminist and postrace ideologies, and both the ways in which "race and gender [are] malleable forces" (Joseph, 2009, p. 238) but also how individuals seek to push and probe these limits in their everyday encounters with racism and sexism. That is, ruptures demonstrate the inevitable tenuousness of post- subjectivity even for Asian American food bloggers who demonstrate their continued investment in its success. The process of reproduction and rupture on Asian American food blogs provides insights into the ways that these dominant discourses are negotiated in the daily practice of identity construction and performance, and in spaces both domestic and digital.

Conclusion

It is clear that food bloggers perform digital identity strategically, with a consciousness of the self-branding strategies that reward greater visibility through demanding anchored and authentic identities, and the presentation of personal narratives as coherent and aligned with frameworks for racial commoditization. One of the main implications of these logics, for Asian American food bloggers, is that race and ethnicity become facts that are always made visible and must be actively performed through a combination of images, descriptions, and symbols, although food bloggers adopt a diverse range of strategies in response, some of which I have outlined in this chapter. This point underscores what has already long been disproven as a feature of the early internet, which is that physical identity markers do not become irrelevant or invisible in digital culture, although the forced visibility of race and the need to justify its value within the blogosphere is also only true for non-white food bloggers. Moreover, given the compulsory ways in which race is incorporated into the self-brand, it is most common for race to be commoditized as difference, given the ways that such an approach is normalized in commercial media and valued within foodie culture.

While I do not fault individual bloggers for adopting this logical strategy, the lack of alternatives that Asian American bloggers have available to them for self-expression in the commercialized food blogosphere explains the reproduction and amplification of hegemonic narratives. Certainly, there are ways that difference is figured in extremely useful ways, particularly given mainstream Western media which have largely overlooked Asian diasporic and immigrant narratives, and have reduced Asian American femininity to a series of exaggerated and unflattering caricatures. Food bloggers embark on a project that utilizes the conventions of the food blogosphere to portray the ways that race is significantly embedded throughout the domestic and routine lives of Asian American women, and the ways that racial identities are highly nuanced, partial, and complex. Nevertheless, there is a constant negotiation with the commercial logics that reinscribe difference as Otherness, and Otherness as valuable only through its exoticization.

In this environment, what I advocate is an analytical approach that is more pragmatic than tasking food bloggers with the somewhat herculean mission of voicing radical political activism through food content, or even looking for subtle or everyday subversions – particularly in a political landscape so irrevocably marked by ambivalence and contradiction – and involves identifying ruptures in the re-production of idealized citizenship. In this chapter, I have outlined the ways that ruptures in the food blogosphere have worked to give food bloggers the opportunity to 'speak back' to some of the racial microaggressions they regularly encounter, drawing attention to these incidents that literally disrupt the reproduction of the postfeminist, postrace subjects that are otherwise painstakingly performed.

References

Ang, I. (2001). *On not speaking Chinese: Living between Asia and the West.* Routledge. 10.4324/9780203996492

Appadurai, A. (1988). How to make a National cuisine: Cookbooks in contemporary India. *Comparative Studies in Society and History, 30*(1), 3–24. 10.1017/S0010417500015024

Avakian, A. (2014). Cooking up lives: Feminist food memoirs. *Feminist Studies, 40*(2), 277–303. 10.1353/fem.2014.0022

Banet-Weiser, S. (2012). *Authentic TM: The politics of ambivalence in a brand culture.* New York University Press.

Baumgardner, J., & Richards, A. (2010). *Manifesta: Young women, feminism, and the future.* Farrar, Straus and Giroux.

Baym, N. K. (2015). Connect with your audience! The relational labor of connection, *The Communication Review, 18*(1), 14–22. 10.1080/10714421.2015.996401

Bell, D., & Hollows, J. (2007). Mobile homes. *Space and Culture, 10*(1), 22–39. 10.1177/1206331206296380

Counihan, C. (2018). Mexicanas' food voice and differential consciousness in the San Luis Valley of Colorado. In C. Counihan, P. Van Esterik, & A. Julier. (Eds.), *Food and Culture* (pp. 191–204). Routledge.

Dejmanee, T. (2016). "Food Porn" as postfeminist play: Digital femininity and the female body on food blogs. *Television & New Media, 17*(5), 429–448. 10.1177/1527476415615944

DeVault, M. (1994). *Feeding the family: The social organization of caring as gendered work*. University of Chicago Press.

Dobson, A. S. (2015). *Postfeminist digital cultures: Femininity, social media, and self-representation*. Palgrave Macmillan. 10.1057/9781137404206

Epp, M. (2015). Eating across borders: Reading Immigrant cookbooks. *Histoire sociale/Social History, 48*(96), 45–65. 10.1353/his.2015.0007.

Hayles, K. (2007). Narrative and database: Natural symbionts. *PMLA: Publications of the Modern Language Association of America, 122*(5), 1603–1608. 10.1632/S0030812900168580

Hearn, A. (2008). Meat, mask, burden: Probing the contours of the branded self. *Journal of Consumer Culture, 8*(2), 197–217. 10.1177/1469540508090086

Ho, A. (n.d.a.). About. *Constellation Inspiration*. https://constellationinspiration.com/about

Ho, A. (n.d.b.). Asian-Inspired. *Constellation Inspiration*. https://constellationinspiration.com/category/asian-inspired

Ho, A. (2020, October 24). Halloween brown sugar breakfast tarts. *Constellation Inspiration*. https://constellationinspiration.com/2020/10/halloween-brown-sugar-breakfast-tarts.html

Ho, A. (2021, February 8). Grilled chewy rice cake. *Constellation Inspiration*. https://constellationinspiration.com/2021/02/grilled-chewy-rice-cake.html

hooks, b. (1992). Eating the other: Desire and resistance. In b. hooks (Ed.), *Black looks: Race and representation* (pp. 21–39). South End.

Inness, S. A. (2001). *Dinner roles: American women and culinary culture*. University of Iowa.

Inness, S. A. (2006). *Secret ingredients: Race, gender, and class at the dinner table*. Palgrave Macmillan.

Itoh, M. (2006, August 9). Back to Japanese basics: The essential staples of a Japanese pantry. *Just Hungry*. https://justhungry.com/2006/08/back_to_japanes.html

Itoh, M. (2008a, December 18). The Japanese food and cooking lexicon. *Just Hungry*. https://justhungry.com/just-hungry-reference-handbooks/japanese-food-and-cooking-lexicon

Itoh, M. (2008b, August 15). About Japanese ingredients and substitutions. *Just Hungry*. https://justhungry.com/about-japanese-ingredients-and-substitutions

Itoh, M. (2008c, January 25). Japanese grocery stores in the United States and territories. *Just Hungry*. https://justhungry.com/handbook/just-hungry-handbooks/japanese-grocery-store-list/united-states

Itoh, M. (2010, September 21). The just hungry FAQ. *Just Hungry*. https://justhungry.com/faq

Itoh, M. (2012, August 24). Basics: Japanese soy sauce – All you need to know (and then some). *Just Hungry*. https://justhungry.com/handbook/just-hungry-handbooks/basics-japanese-soy-sauce-all-you-need-know

Johnston, J., & Baumann, S. (2010). *Foodies: Democracy and distinction in the gourmet foodscape*. Routledge.

Joseph, R. (2009). "Tyra Banks is fat": Reading (post-)racism and (post-)feminism in the new millennium. *Critical Studies in Media Communication, 26*(3), 237–254. 10.1080/15295030903015096

Kinder, M. (2002). Hot spots, avatars, and narrative fields forever: Buññuel's legacy for new digital media and interactive database narrative. *Film Quarterly, 55*(4), 2–15. 10.1525/fq.2002.55.4.2

Kristeva, J., Jardine, A., & Blake, H. (1981). Women's time. *Signs, 7*(1), 13–35. http://www.jstor.org/stable/3173503

Le Dantec-Lowry, H. (2008). Reading women's lives in cookbooks and other culinary writings: A critical essay. *Revue Française D'études Américaines, 116*(2), 99–122. 10.3917/rfea.116.0099

Leonardi, S. (1989). Recipes for reading: Summer pasta, lobster à la riseholme, and key lime pie. *PMLA: Publications of the Modern Language Association of America, 104*(3), 340–347. 10.2307/462443

Lillian. (n.d.) About. *Chinese Grandma*. https://chinesegrandma.com/about/

Lillian. (2010, July 26). The real Chinese grandmas. *Chinese Grandma*. https://chinesegrandma.com/2010/07/the-real-chinese-grandmas/

Lillian. (2016, March 15). Chinese takeout chicken (less the grease/guilt). *Chinese Grandma*. https://chinesegrandma.com/2016/03/chinese-takeout-chicken/

Ma, S. M. (1998). *Immigrant Subjectivities in Asian American and Asian Diaspora Literatures*. SUNY.

Mannur, A. (2013). Eat, dwell, orient: Food networks and Asian/American cooking communities, *Cultural Studies, 27*(4), 585–610. 10.1080/09502386.2012.725060

Manovich, L. (2000). *The language of new media*. MIT Press.

McFeely, M. D. (2001). *Can she bake a cherry pie?: American women and the kitchen in the twentieth century*. University of Massachusetts.

Negra, D. (2002). Ethnic food fetishism, whiteness, and nostalgia in recent film and television. *Velvet Light Trap*. https://link.gale.com/apps/doc/A952-62639/LitRC?u=anon~2eb0d307&sid=googleScholar&xid=f68261ed

Negra, D. (2009). *What a girl wants?: Fantasizing the reclamation of self in postfeminism*. Routledge.

Neuhaus, J. (1999). The way to a man's heart: Gender roles, domestic ideology, and cookbooks in the 1950s. *Journal of Social History, 32*(3), 529–555. 10.1353/jsh/32.3.529

Pham, M. H. T. (2015). *Asians wear clothes on the Internet: Race, gender, and the work of personal style blogging*. Duke University Press.

Shapiro, L. (1986). *Perfection salad: Women and cooking at the turn of the century*. University of California Press.

Theophano, J. (2002). *Eat my words: Reading women's lives through the cookbooks they wrote*. Palgrave.
Tye, D. (2010). *Baking as biography: A life in recipes*. McGill-Queens University Press.
Yeh, M. (n.d.). About. *My Name is Yeh.* https://mynameisyeh.com/about
Zafar, R. (1999). The signifying dish: Autobiography and history in two Black women's cookbooks. *Feminist Studies, 25*(2), 449–469. 10.2307/3178690

3 Comments, Community and Controversy: Imagining the Asian American Audience

In early 2021 Tieghan Gerard, a white American food blogger who boasts millions of online followers (Tu, 2021), posted a recipe on her blog titled 'Weeknight Ginger Chicken Pho Ga (Vietnamese chicken soup)' (2021). Gerard acknowledges that the recipe is inspired by Vietnamese pho before offering her 'improvements' to this centuries-old dish: "I wanted something a bit lighter. So I tried to recreate a pho with crispy roasted chicken, noodles, and broth. It's just as delicious, but slightly lighter, and simpler to make at home!" Vietnamese American and other readers objected to Gerard's characterization of this recipe as pho, both due to her addition of ingredients that are not found in pho (including crispy roasted chicken, soy sauce, sesame oil, garlic, honey and wheat noodles), her lack of attention to the historical and cultural contexts of this dish, and her insinuation that her recipe is an improvement on this Vietnamese dish. This recipe generated many polarized opinions which were published on the blog post. Several comments articulated the view that Gerard's recipe amounted to whitewashing and cultural appropriation and that it was inaccurate to call this recipe pho. Other commenters mocked the recipe's bizarre adaptations and expressed their anger toward Gerard and her dismissive response to concerned Vietnamese American readers. Alternatively, commenters defended Gerard by presenting her as an innocent victim of 'cancel culture,' affirming her character as 'nice' and 'good' while denigrating her critics as whiny, pathetic, and themselves racist. Dismissive commenters also described the criticism of this recipe as oversensitive. Ultimately, Gerard changed the title of this post but otherwise refused to remove or apologize for her recipe and narrative.

In a postrace environment where race is often referenced as a property divorced from history and structural power relations, Gerard's controversial pho recipe was viewed as a fuss over nothing by those who accepted its colorblind framing as a question of adaptation

DOI: 10.4324/9781003302278-3

or authenticity. After all, adaptations of recipes are common across the food blogosphere and, as long as they are properly credited, are often expected and even welcomed due to the potential for cross-promotion. The history of food and recipe adaptation led to many commenters drawing false analogies (and false generalizations) about Italian Americans not being upset about French bread pizza, or 'Mexican Americans' not complaining about the various ways that tacos have been adapted in the United States. Similarly, some commenters defending this recipe misunderstood this as a controversy about authenticity. In foodie culture, authenticity is often understood as appealing to historical and locally-specific non-Western geographies, which often sets up a false and problematic binary between the cosmopolitan, white Western foodie and the exoticized Other who is assumed to be fixed in place and time (Bell & Hollows, 2007). Within the food blogosphere, claims to authenticity are often made through drawing on heritage and experience, with many Asian American food bloggers successfully drawing on race to implicitly support the credibility and perceived authenticity of their recipes. However, heritage and experience are just one form of transferring food pedagogies, and there are many non-Asian bloggers who publish carefully researched, contextualized and credited Asian recipes and blogs. While Gerard's glib description of pho is exasperating, it is not itself the issue and in fact becomes the basis for her self-defense as she suggests that her description of pho as Vietnamese provides the context that absolves her from accusations of cultural appropriation. Moreover, racial heritage is also used to seemingly legitimate racist commentary about the issue with commenters self-identifying themselves as Italian and Australian to demonstrate how they are 'beyond' what they characterize as the petty and trivial concerns of outspoken Vietnamese Americans. Some other Asian American commenters self-identify as Vietnamese American and Filipino to voice the threat that continuing to 'make a fuss' over incidents such as this will threaten the model minority status of Asian Americans.

Instead, the issue is rightly one of cultural appropriation, where white oppressors systematically appropriate the cultural knowledge and objects of non-white Others for personal commercial gain, a stance that demands both a historical understanding of the racialized power dynamics and racial history of the United States and a foregrounding of race – both of which are denied by postrace discourse – to understand. From this perspective, it is clear that Gerard's cultural appropriation of Asian dishes is entrenched as part of her blog's brand strategy. A cursory look through her blog includes recipes titled 'Better

Than Dan Dan Noodles' a 'Quick Kale and Mushroom Pho' and 'Weeknight Thai Chicken Meatball Khao Soi' in which Gerard posts a perfunctory sentence about these Asian dishes before positing her own 'superior' versions of these recipes, often colonizing these dishes – or adding original twists, in food blog speak – to suit the fashions for healthism and efficiency in the Western kitchen by noting that her versions are healthier, lighter, easier and quicker to make. This power dynamic is exacerbated through her large following as a food blogger, a position in which her whiteness is highly consequential. In the interplay of the postfeminist and postrace logics with which food blogs are imbricated, the 'nice' white femininity of the food blogosphere – which was used by commenters to defend Gerard's character – is also deployed to authorize racism on her site for instance in her sweet response to the racist comment by 'A Friend' who writes: "Where do you think the baguette for Bahn [sic] Mi came from? Hint: not originally vietnam. [sic] Food is boundless. No race or culture owns it because it is art" (2021) to which Gerard responds: "Thanks so much for your positive feedback and kind message:) xTieghan" (2021).

This example presents one understanding of how the contentious issue of racism and cultural appropriation is discussed on food blogs, particularly through the comments section which is one of the primary sections of a food blog where the blogger and her audience publicly co-construct and negotiate the meanings of these digital texts. While commenters are only a small fraction of a food blog's audience, and readers who choose to comment are not necessarily representative of the wider audience base, comments as digital traces amplify certain discourses and make hypervisible particular networked publics. Accordingly, this chapter focuses on comments as indicators of how Asian American food blogs center certain imagined communities and structure possibilities for political and racial dialogue. I explore the ways that close imagined communities in the food blogosphere often arise as a function of gendered disclosures, and how the comment curation strategies of Asian American food bloggers suggest that content is oriented toward a predominantly white imagined audience.

The Imagined Community of the Food Blogosphere

Community is central to the food blogosphere, and food blogs encode the personal bonds and communities forged through food work and food writing, building on the recipe's inherent connotations of exchange (Leonardi, 1989) as well as the social relationships developed around the production and consumption of food (McFeely, 2001; Tye, 2010).

Food blogs foster connection through the circulation of both food knowledge and personal intimacies, exchanges that generate a gift economy where food and domestic pedagogies are archived, indexed and searchable, serving as a valuable resource for a broader community of people engaged in food work. Several food bloggers have described the blogosphere as a site where close bonds are forged between food bloggers and readers. Rosie Alyea writes that within the food blogging community: "there is a camaraderie and connection that I simply wouldn't believe possible if I wasn't part of it all" (2011) while Kelly Yandell shares that food bloggers: "have a new kind of community that transcends geography and family" (2011). The fact that these online discourses and communities emerging from the food and lifestyle blogospheres have often centered around women participants and stereotypically female-gendered experiences have been used to support arguments for the blogosphere's political potential. Emily Matchar argues that lifestyle blogs are the "online versions of the knitting circles and quilting bees of preindustrial America" (2013, p. 52) and Jessalynn Keller (2012) argues that girls' feminist blogs provide a site for girls to gather and share personal experiences in a manner reminiscent of 1970s feminist consciousness raising groups. Lori Lopez (2009) describes mommy blogging as a 'radical act' due to the way these texts invite solidarity and validation among mothers and allow women to define motherhood and identity in their own voices. Moreover, many studies based on interviews with bloggers have emphasized the social support that arises through women's blogging communities including 'healthy' food blogs (Lynch, 2010), fashion blogs (Marwick, 2013), and mommy blogs (Makinen, 2021). Over the years, the food blogosphere has proven to be effective at drawing on mundane exchanges of intimacy over time to generate a climate in which more profound gendered experiences could be shared and discussed. For instance, the food blogosphere has rallied around personal upheavals shared by bloggers including coming out as a middle-age lesbian (Wizenberg, 2016), grappling with the traumatic experience of stillbirth (Ostrom, 2017), the grief of unexpected widowhood (Perillo, 2011), and countless stories of divorce. While these posts are not common across the blogosphere, they have contributed to building online communities of support and acceptance that form around life changes and traumatic experiences, most of which revolve around ruptures to the normative heterosexual milestones of marriage and the nuclear family. These findings support the notion that communities and cultures centered around women's blogging practices can operate as a form of everyday feminist praxis.

Outside of the food and lifestyle blogospheres, a parallel set of studies have detailed how online forums provide critical spaces for Asian American and Asian diasporic communities and counterpublics to gather, find mutual understanding and support, discuss identity politics, and engage in political activism. David Parker and Miri Song (2006) study two community websites where British South Asian and British Chinese individuals gather to banter, share culturally-specific information, and engage in discussions around identity politics that Parker and Song characterize as 'reflective racialization', in which digital communication affordances are used to host "self-authored commentary on the issues faced by racialized minorities in a multicultural context" (2006, p. 583). This space allows British South Asian and Chinese communities to discuss concepts of ethnic identity, authenticity and belonging, gain community support, and explore the fluidity of racial identity. Crystal Abidin and Jing Zeng (2020) analyze the Facebook group Subtle Asian Traits, whose Asian diasporic community members circulate strategies including catharsis, escalation and problem solving in response to racism during the covid-19 pandemic. Lori Lopez examines Asian American blogs which she argues work to construct "an Asian American counterpublic wherein this marginalized community has the opportunity to talk about shared values and experiences, challenging their silencing within the public sphere" (2014, p. 424). Meanwhile, Dasol Kim describes the ways that Asian American beauty vloggers are able to generate a community of Asian American followers, who become visible through likes and comments on videos and work to create "an intimate and affective space for Asian American viewers to construct what may be called 'online sisterhood' based on their shared racialized experiences" (2021, p. 10). A common thread noted in these groups is that while politics and activism are rarely imagined as the sole or even primary purpose of these communities, through the exchange of more mundane banter and frivolous cultural references or experiences, bonds of trust and an infrastructure for Asian American and diasporic community are built and can be swiftly mobilized towards discussions of racism and political action, as well as for generating meaningful Asian American political spaces, dialogue and communities through digital platforms and cultures. These digital cultures also explicitly demarcate their issues as specifically relevant to Asian American and Asian diasporic communities.

However, despite this evidence detailing the feminist potential for building supportive communities around lifestyle and food blogs, as well as the body of research on the formation of engaged Asian American political communities, an intersectional analysis of Asian American food blogs reveals that these texts rarely center Asian American identity politics or make visible specifically Asian American communities. In her study of Asian American bloggers, Lori Lopez (2014) distinguishes between bloggers who "happen to be Asian American but blog on specific topics such as politics, food, parenting, or technology" (p. 422) and the "distinct and flourishing category of Asian American bloggers who focus on the topic of Asian America ... cover[ing] news items and writ[ing] personal stories that relate to a broader political notion of an interconnected Asian American community" (p. 422). I concur with the significance of this difference and explore the ways that even though Asian American food bloggers center the quotidian experiences of their racial and gendered identities in a manner that has yielded productive feminist dialogue and community, these performances and texts are less successful at producing productive and visible racial dialogue for food bloggers who 'happen to be' Asian American. For instance, in a statement on her About page, Chen McTernan of *Two Red Bowls* writes: "All that I know I learned from my mother, grandmother, mother-in-law, and the Internet," tracing a lineage from her Chinese mother and grandmother to the broader Internet community that obfuscates race in favour of promoting an imagined gendered community. Drawing on danah boyd's concept of networked publics as "the imagined collective that emerges as a result of the intersection of people, technology, and practice" (2011, p. 39), I explore how blog comments, as an important part of the site architecture for this genre, structure dialogue and imagined community in a way that variously amplifies and obfuscates certain discourses about food, gender, and race.

Imagining Audience through Food Blog Comments

A recipe for homemade oat milk on *Oh She Glows,* a health food blog created by white Canadian blogger Angela Liddon, generates a slew of impassioned comments from readers who draw on Liddon's narrative and recipe to engage in lively dialogue on the perils of carrageenan and GMOs, the dangers of fillers, synthetic vitamins and arsenic lurking in commercial brands of almond milk, the ethics, business practices and relative virtues and vices of different alternative milk brands on the market (Liddon, 2013). A small sample of commenters include 'Carie' who advises readers to look out for the Silk Pure Almond brand of milk which does not contain carrageenan (2013), to which 'Klaine' responds that Blue Diamond is preferable as unlike Silk brand milks it is GMO-free (2013). 'Nikki' refutes Klaine's suggestion by pointing out that while Silk is GMO-free, it is owned by dairy agribusiness Dean Foods (2013). 'Sarah' offers that she and her family drink Rice Dream in order to avoid carrageenan (2013), to which 'Vicky' responds that rice milk contains "huge amount of arsenic (yes, the poison!) ... Google 'Arsenic in rice' and you'll see!" (2014).

This thread demonstrates how the comments sections of food blogs can be used to host political dialogue and debate, with this example centered around community discussion of 'ethical food discourses,' in which conscientious consumption and "personal shopping choices ... are directed toward improving the public good alongside individual well-being" (Cairns et al., 2013). This discourse is steeped in neoliberal individualist rhetoric and an attention to 'healthism' – in which health is considered a moral virtue that arises from the individual's personal diligence in enacting 'healthy' lifestyle practices (Crawford, 1980), both of which are dominant ideologies circulated within the food blogosphere. While blogger Liddon hosts this thread, the comment exchange demonstrates how food blogs serve as space where readers can debate the nuances of food and health discourses and, in doing so, build a lively community of readers around the food blog. In this particular example, commenters appear to exacerbate rather than resolve the anxieties that burden individual food preparers in this climate, and to encourage rather than critique the gendered, individual burdens of labor implicit in ethical food discourse. Yet, this thread nevertheless provides a rare site where individuals can exchange commentary, information and advice that make salient the impact of these food discourses on their lived experiences.

While similar exchanges appear across the food blogosphere, the form of these comment discussions and dialogue is shaped by a number of architectural and generic conventions. First, comments are governed by the practice of moderation, which food bloggers routinely engage in at their discretion, shaping the kinds of feedback discourses made visible on their blogs. Such moderation practices generally fall in line with what bloggers describe as 'hosting' readers meaning that the site is meant to feel welcoming to as broad a readership as possible, which is used to justify the general practice of steering clear of explicit discussion of politics or controversial topics, an ethos that also aligns with best-practices for commercial lifestyle media. While most online communities and forums have moderation practices, typically these are published for and accessible to the community. In contrast, food bloggers have unilateral control over their moderation practices and are generally not beholden to their audience to publish or justify these practices. Second, very few readers ever post comments on food blogs, meaning that these interactions are not necessarily representative of the general readership of any given blog, although they serve to make visible the possibilities for community that form around these blogs. Third, blog comments have long had a transactional function within the food blogging community, used for cross-promotional purposes alongside blogrolls and shared links that make visible bloggers' positioning within the networked food blogosphere, meaning that they are often considered "sociable in that they serve more to affirm the relationship than to convey information" (Ryan, 2018, p. 175). Accordingly, while comments are user-generated, the blogger shapes the possibilities for hosting dialogue and community through their control over site architecture and moderation.

Comments on food blogs reflect the dynamism of the digital blog post, functioning as a space that makes visible publicly performed interactions between the blogger and her readers. As a result, commenting practices can be imagined as an ongoing negotiation between the food blogger and her readership and, in turn, how this construction of online community shapes the possibilities for political dialogue. Despite their curation and partial representation of audience, comments are nevertheless indicative of the important ways that the blogger's persona and brand is co-constituted through their relationship to their *imagined audience*. Audiences in online spaces are characterized through 'context collapse' where multiple audiences – such as professional and personal acquaintances – are flattened through digital platforms (Marwick & boyd, 2011). However, even though a food blog will invariably host diverse readers as audiences, online communications are always directed toward a particular imagined audience (Marwick & boyd, 2011) and for food bloggers, as with all digital influencers, this imagined audience is constructed with reference to the commoditization of an online following (Hunter, 2016). While commercialization does not inherently negate the political possibilities of an online text or culture, the logics of visibility and the aspirational performance of lifestyle through which food blogs gain commercial viability delimit the tenor and form of political commentary and dialogue that is possible. This is demonstrated by Suuronen, Reinkainen, Borchers and Strandberg's (2021) study of Finnish social media influencers that found while the majority of influencers mentioned politics on their platforms, typically this was expressed through lifestyle-based narratives – most commonly on the topics of consumer behavior, health and eating, and climate change – and influencers with more brand collaborations were more likely to discuss political topics, potentially because they were more established in their field and more likely to weather the risks of speaking out. The comments section of food blogs stands as a visible and public negotiation of the possibilities and delimitations of political dialogue and imagined community.

Food blogs have often navigated context collapse with a preference for articulating the imagined audience through the 'sister test,' adopting a tone of assumed intimacy even though the readership of any given food blog is likely to be largely unknown. As blogger Ree Drummond writes, this understanding of readers as 'sisters' guides the kinds of content and tone used on the blog, as she offers in a post meant to serve as a guide to aspiring food bloggers: "I tend to blog about the same things I'd talk to my sister about ... .[and] I tend not to blog about things I wouldn't talk to my sister about" (2010). The 'sister test' serves the purpose of monetizing food blogs, as ongoing communications of authenticity and intimacy build relationships of trust between bloggers and readers that become the foundation for bloggers' successful product endorsements and brand partnerships (Matchar, 2013). However, the 'sister test' ultimately prescribes an inherently white sisterhood in Western contexts, for whom knowledge of Asian food pedagogies, techniques and ingredients must typically be translated for rather than assumed by the blogger, and mundane experiences of the Asian identity are presented in unequivocally positive terms. That is, the commercialized imagined audience limits the visibility of Asian American politics as Asian American readers rarely constitute the primary imagined audience for these texts. Instead, commenting patterns on Asian American food blogs elucidate the strategic ways that the imagined audience is constructed as a relationship between the reader and blogger. Commenting practices also reveal the reliance on gendered, domestic, and postfeminist experiences as structuring the bonds of intimacy with, and the bounds of, the imagined audience while conversely, race is absent as a shared characteristic imagined between the blogger and her audience.

Comment Curation on Asian American Food Blogs

Having established that comments make visible political dialogue that is negotiated within the architecture of a food blog, the moderation and hosting capabilities of the food blogger, and the participation of commenters, I further explore this through the study of comment curation styles on Asian American food blogs. Three distinct comment curation styles emerge, suggesting an intentionality with which community engagement is fostered as part of the brand strategy of food blogs. Even though comments are generated by the audience, food bloggers shape this dialogue through the comments that they choose to publish, respond to and ignore. The three categories are not mutually exclusive, and there is an inherent messiness to the commenting process – comments can be missed, unruly, spam, misunderstandings. However, most blogs unequivocally lean towards one of the styles detailed below – the helper, the close friend, and the creative community – and the kinds of comments that appear on posts are generally easy to classify within one of these categories, underlining the consistent and considered ways in which food blog comments work to make salient a commercialized, imagined audience that is compatible with the brand of the food blog.

The 'helper' style provides detailed feedback to comments about recipe content including instruction clarifications, substitutions, reviews after making the recipes. For example, on the blog *Wild Wild Whisk*, Trang Doan responds dutifully and meticulously to the large number of specific questions posted on her popular 'Mini Chocolate Cake' recipe, such as how differently-sized cake tins would change the baking time, substituting gluten free and self-raising flours in the recipe, using butter instead of oil, and whether buttermilk can be left out of the recipe as well as many favorable reviews (2020). Her detailed response to the question of whether buttermilk can be substituted for water:

> You can, but I recommend using buttermilk for more richness or use regular milk. If you don't use buttermilk in this recipe, you must use natural cocoa powder because baking soda needs something acidic. If you only have dutch-process cocoa powder and using water, you need to substitute the baking soda for baking powder.
>
> (Doan, 2020)

coheres with the *Wild Wild Whisk* brand, which develops a precise and scientific approach to baking through detailed explanations of baking processes, tips and hints. It also positions Doan as an expert who cultivates a democratic relationship to the audience through her accessibility on the comments page and her friendly, encouraging and considered responses to the audience, a gendered form of emotional labour that is essential to influencers' performances of authenticity (Van Driel & Dumitrica, 2021).

The 'close friend' commenting style imagines readers as an extended network of friends and family, often drawing on female life milestones and domestic experiences as the imagined universalized foundations for intimacy with and relatability to the imagined audience. For instance, on the post 'Life Lately,' Chen McTernan's announcement of her third pregnancy generates personalized praise and congratulations from unknown commenters (2021). Commenter 'Emily' writes:

> Luke and Clara [Chen McTernan's older children] are getting so big!!! I enjoyed reading about your life update–I hope your pregnancy gets easier and that your morning sickness ends soon! I hope you and your family continue to be safe and healthy during this crazy times. Thank you for the update and I look forward to hearing more news in the future!
>
> (2021)

to which Chen McTernan responds:

> Thank you so much, Emily! It is already getting lots better, and I'm already working on a few little things in the hopper (it's really been awhile, I almost forgot how to blog!) so all good things and so appreciate you still being here
>
> (Chen, 2021)

an exchange that suggests a relationship of friendship and support though the added detail 'appreciate you still being here' subtly alludes to the value generated on food blogs through the commercialization of friends as followers, and the idea that the basis for this online relationship in fact hinges on relational labor (Baym, 2015), and the blogger's compulsory ongoing communication of intimacies through regularly updated content.

The 'creative community' style employs comments to make visible the connections of the blogger within a creative community of fellow food bloggers. This can be seen on the blog *Betty Liu* where blogger Liu publishes only a small number of comments, the majority of which are written by other prominent food bloggers. Such comment curation establishes a community of prominent bloggers who bond over their shared respect and admiration of each other's creative practices, emphasizing the art and technical skills of food blogging in line with Liu's blog which has been recognized for its award-winning food photography and videography as well as for showcasing unique flavour combinations such as miso oatmeal and black sesame seed fried chicken. Liu further builds bonds within this creative community by cooking and featuring recipes from fellow blogger's cookbooks. The cross-promotional comments that appear on Liu's site include the name of bloggers and their blogs/brands as well as sometimes a link to their own food blogs, and comment favorably on other blogger's posts, photography and recipes. In this commenting practice, there is cachet attached to commenting early as soon as posts are dropped, ensuring that questions about substitutions or reviews are almost never published, but indicating that the commenting blogger is highly attuned to the latest developments within the food blogging community. Many of the bloggers who comment feature on multiple posts, further underlining Betty's personal relationships and mutual admiration of the work of these other bloggers, and the focus on this support as part of an ongoing online community built upon the support and exchange of creative skills and technical knowledge specific to food blogging.

In addition to the ways that these comment curation patterns reveal how these sites for audience engagement in the food blogosphere are structured by brand strategy, they also detail how imagined audiences are positioned relationally to the food blogger in ways that emphasize gender. These three styles demonstrate a preference for drawing on heteronormative feminine, domestic experiences that are assumed to be universal amongst the imagined audience, and highlight the postfeminist capacity of the food blogger. The style of generating 'helper' and 'close friend' comments, and the willingness to respond to commenters and exchange pedagogical knowledge and personal intimacies, approximates the self-disclosure strategies of female friendships (Bane et al., 2010) and is a site for enacting 'feminized' relational labor, the service-oriented, immaterial labor designed to regulate emotional responses that demands performances of social, emotional and domestic femininity (Baym, 2015). The conjoining of feminine performance with commercial strategy is also made explicit through 'creative curation' which works to highlight the postfeminist capacity through entrepreneurialism and the gendered ideals inherent to the romanticized creative economy (McRobbie, 2016; Duffy, 2017). Inversely, the positioning of the food blogger and her imagined audience are racially non-specific, and race is generally only made explicit in terms that require translation and explanation rather than forming the grounds of solidarity with the imagined audience. For instance, the use of the identifier 'Asian' across these texts is almost always limited to a lifestyle attribute, foreclosing the possibility of discussions of the experiences of race and racism that might expand an understanding of 'Asian' beyond the consumable and commodifiable.

Such an outcome is distinctly strategic given the commercialization of the food blog audience. Assuming that heteronormative gendered experiences form the grounds for audience relatability aligns with commercial lifestyle media's orientation towards white female consumers, favoring the blogger's ability to attract partnerships and sponsorships. However, this appeal to a broadly commercialized gendered audience detracts from the race-based intimacies that would support the formation of a more narrowly defined yet politically charged Asian American community. As danah boyd writes, "knowing one's audience matters when trying to determine what is socially appropriate to say or what will be understood by those listening. In other words, audience is critical to context" (2010, p. 50) and it is reasonable to assume that the white imagined audience would have the effect of muting dialogue about structural racism, for instance, which might alienate a non-Asian American audience by triggering white guilt or white fragility. While the commercialization of a following is not inherently incompatible with the cultivation of political dialogue on food and lifestyle blogs, the commercial logics of food blogs prioritize an imagined audience based on heteronormative, hegemonic feminine subject and her assumed lifestyle and interests, even when the bloggers are Asian American. Comments – through their visibility and structured avenues for audience engagement – then amplify and reinforce these cultural norms within the food blogosphere.

Desperately Seeking the (Asian American) Audience

Ien Ang's (1991) book, *Desperately Seeking the Audience*, forwards critical arguments against the institutionally-defined, commercial construction of the television audiences as a homogenous mass. In the present study, it is similarly worth remembering that even though the cultivated imagined audience of the food blogosphere is white, the food blog audience is ultimately diverse and the critical interpretations they bring to Asian American food blogs are polysemous. While there are significant impediments to generating Asian American community in the food blogosphere, where this community and Asian American identity politics are made visible on Asian American food blogs, they appear as ruptures in the postrace logics that serve as the foundations for these brands. One such moment takes place on the foundational post on *Chinese Grandma* in which Lillian introduces her 'real' Chinese Grandmas (2010) and in turn inspires several comments from Asian American readers. For example, 'AliceK' writes:

> I immigrated to the US when I was 9 and it has been over 40 years now. I am trying to duplicate my mother's steamed cake recipe. I regret not learning from her how to cook/make traditional

Chinese food when she was still here with us. It's been over 13 years since she's been gone. I have searched everywhere online and have tried many recipes. I have not been able to re-create the steamed sponge cake – the way she made it.

(2013)

'Doreen' comments:

Came across your website after a rather grey, soberly discussion with my colleague that as a Chinese working mother in Asia, I have hardly made anything in the kitchen that came close to the scent of growing up in my own mama's kitchen – of hainanese style coffee, steamed sponge cake, steamed chicken rice and etc.

(2013)

'Kiyuu' adds this comment to Chinese Grandma's post:

came here via googling 'chinese oatmeal,' haha, I've got to try some of those ideas. I'm commenting because I saw a connexion between both our grandparents, which was pretty interesting. My paternal grandparents were both from Shandong, and fled during the revolution. My grandfather, to Japan, for education, then Taiwan, and my Grandmother's family to Korea (they lived there and China equally, anyway, so the transition was fairly easy) and then fled again, to Taiwan!

(2011)

While 'Jourdie' writes:

As the proud granddaughter of an awesome Chinese grandma, this history and recognition actually made me tear up. Yay for heritage and tenacity and the shareable, edible traditions!

(2014)

These spontaneous testimonies perform visibility politics, momentarily amplifying and centering the Asian American experience. These comments demonstrate how Lillian's post generates affective responses for Asian American readers, and the mutual support that arises through articulating and sharing these histories of Asian migration to the United States which are rarely made visible in Western media and cultural spaces. The reader testimonies work to affirm the shared solidarity of this Asian American community, while also making clear the historical and contextual differences that represent the diversity of Asian American experiences. Kiyuu's references to the specific historical and geographical details about his family's migration to the United States support Lillian's post's work in giving life to and individualizing Asian American people and families that pushes back against the dehumanizing stereotypes and homogeneity with which Asian Americans are often portrayed in US media and the cultural imaginary. AliceK and Doreen's comments offer a gendered perspective on the immigrant experience, highlighting the themes of loss which are punctuated through the breaks it creates in maternal practices – the inability to recreate their mother's cooking can be read more broadly as a sense of loss of cultural tradition and history that inevitably takes place through immigration. These melancholic testimonies punctuate the generally cheerful and upbeat tone of the food blogosphere. Moreover, this critical mass of comments appears in response to the post which explicitly outlines Lillian's postrace framing of her Chinese heritage, and their similar emphasis on real-life immigration stories – and the specific experiences of their Chinese grandmas – ground race in historical and geographical materialities, rejecting the postrace positioning of Chinese as a mere lifestyle and personal characteristic.

A second way in which Asian American community is made visible is through highlighting connections and exchanges between Asian American food bloggers. This takes place readily through the functions of the food blog platform wherein cross-promotion and link acknowledgements are common. For instance, in a post for 'Black Sesame Karaage Chicken' (Liu, 2019), Liu references two fellow Asian American bloggers, Mandy from *Lady and Pups* and Nami from *Just One Cookbook*, who have influenced her recipe and creative work. Similarly, in a post for rose and lychee mooncakes on *Two Red Bowls* (Chen, 2021), Chen McTernan credits the work of Amy from *Constellation Inspiration* and Nami from *Just One Cookbook*. This networked visibility is also highlighted through the messages of support posted as comments by fellow Asian American food bloggers. This practice performs the due diligence of referencing and acknowledging colleagues within the food blogosphere, but also generates a traceable network of Asian American bloggers which, within the attention economy of the food blogosphere, doubles as economically supporting the creative work of fellow food bloggers of Asian descent.

However, these networks highlight a knowledge community whose paths are forged through the shared experiences and foodways of Asian American bloggers, emphasizing the particular value of these common race-based experiences of food and culture and making visible a coalition of Asian American food bloggers within the broader blogosphere. Moreover, this exchange and adaptation of specific Asian recipes implicitly reinforces the authority of Asian American food bloggers over pan-Asian recipes, in response to the cultural appropriation that is celebrated, for instance, in Gerard's pho controversy. While these recipes suggest a tolerance of pan-Asian expertise in cooking, the individualized twists inevitably imprinted upon each published recipe demonstrate the uniqueness of Asian American food bloggers, in the same way that Dasol Kim (2021) argues that comparative monolid makeup videos posted by different Asian American beauty vloggers works to focus on the individuality of Asian foods, cultures and individuals that challenges stereotypes of homogeneity. Accordingly, while Asian American communities are rarely the imagined audience of Asian American food bloggers, this community nevertheless makes itself visible at times, challenging the dominant postrace presentation of race in the food blogosphere and highlighting the polysemy of Asian American food blogs.

Conclusion

This exploration of comments and community building reveals that Asian American food blogs rarely generate dialogue and community that is specifically meaningful to Asian American communities. While the comments sections of food blogs can be important sites for communities to gather around knowledge exchange and for discussion around lifestyle politics that may be particularly relevant for gendered discourse and identity, food and health politics and consumer activism, food blogs can be unsuited for hosting productive and active discussions of institutional politics or 'controversial' social topics due to the cultivation of a broad imagined audience and commercially palatable lifestyle content. Moreover, the commercial logics of the food blogosphere prescribe an overt and hyperfeminine performance of gender – for instance through imagining the community as sisters with whom the assumed shared experiences of motherhood, heterosexual marriage and domesticity forms the basis of intimacy and trust – while simultaneously erasing the significance and experience of race as a nuanced and complex way in which identity is negotiated in everyday and domestic life for Asian American women. More broadly, this demonstrates how in the intersection of commercial postfeminist and postrace ideologies, femininity is exaggerated and universalized within a narrow and traditional conception of gender while race is either drawn on as a commodity that imparts a useful difference and 'exoticism' to the white blogosphere but is otherwise erased thematically, as a site of meaningful experience, and as the basis for community. This unsatisfactory outcome significantly qualifies the political potential of Asian American food blogs for generating dialogue and community around Asian American identity politics.

Additionally, comment architecture provides a clumsy space for communal discussion – comments are most often directed specifically to the blogger, a practice which rarely facilitates extensive dialogue between readers. The designation of a food blog as a space where bloggers 'host' their audience may also make readers reluctant to post answers to other commenters, even if they are able to adequately respond, minimizing the potential impact and efficacy of the wisdom of the crowds in this digital culture. Moreover, comments appear below each post and blog page, meaning that meaningful discussion may be dispersed across many pages of a popular food blog. For example, a post in which *Smitten Kitchen* blogger Perelman (2016) speaks out against Trump's election in 2016 is obliquely filed under a post titled 'Root Vegetable Gratin,' effectively meaning that this important political discussion is unlikely to be retrospectively found through an online search or to attract readers who wish to participate in the conversation.

A further point to consider is that although generally only positive and affirmatory comments are published on food blogs, conveying the idealized notion that food blogging fosters warm and intimate connections, the food blogosphere routinely attracts an abundance of spam, trolling and negative attack comments, and food blogging communities are neither uniformly positive nor supportive. Bloggers have expressed the sentiment that as the blogosphere has evolved to become a more streamlined and professionalized commercial environment, the kinds of communities and commentary it attracts has also changed. As Betty Liu writes,

> with the rise of Instagram and then the algorithm changes that have a lot of us not truly reaching our audience, I found myself longing for the blogging days. I yearned for a deeper connection than a few emoticons, short captions, and rapid scrolling. Maybe it's just me, but I feel a disconnect with my community ... Sometimes I feel like my community has shrunk to only the people who actively comment with me.
>
> (2018)

Liu also actively talks about her feeling of burnout from blogging, and the increasing competitiveness and professional requirements to maintain a successful food blog, the sentiments of which are echoed and supported by several fellow bloggers in the comments section. Such ruptures of the affective tone of the blogosphere offer hints as to the deeper emotional burdens carried by individual bloggers. In her discussion of Finnish mommy blogs, Katariina Makinen details the prevalence of abuse and bullying that is routinely directed at mommy bloggers, and how the affective intimacy required of the genre makes these bloggers particularly vulnerable as online attacks "are tied to the personal histories and family situations of the bloggers" (2021, p. 2972). Similarly, Lopez notes that trolling and personal attacks are considered inevitable on Asian American blogs, and for many bloggers "attacks became viciously personal, and could not be tolerated" (2014, p. 431). Inevitably, more and more bloggers have begun to admit to their readers that they cannot maintain the labor of monitoring and responding to comments. Many other bloggers have simply disabled comments on their blog platforms, further removing possibilities for generating productive community and dialogue from their intimate reflections and creating distance but also one-way communication patterns that are increasingly reminiscent of commercial mainstream media.

These arguments present a clear picture of the significant limitations for Asian American community building within the conventions and digital culture of the food blogosphere and, where examples of ruptures occur which offer counterpoints to the notion that Asian American food blogs are unable to generate Asian American community and dialogue, they are nevertheless fleeting, random and spontaneous. Moreover, significant discussions of race and identity politics are partial, shifting, and negotiated within the bounds of neoliberal and commercial discourses. The emergence of such moments as ruptures minimizes the predictability, quantity and impact of this community-building, and does not lead to sustained dialogue around the Asian American experience. As Asian American readers are not the dominant or intended audience for these blogs, they suffer from a general lack of visibility or searchability on these sites which impedes their ability to gather, organize and make their race-based experiences visible within the food blogosphere, denying their utility as potential spaces for political formation. Given these constraints to performing Asian American identity politics through everyday politics, the final two chapters explore how racial dialogue and race-based community building is practiced more overtly through political hashtag activism.

References

A friend. (2021, February 22). "Cultural appropriation" lol. Listen to yourselves. Where do you think the baguette for Bahn Mi came from? Hint: not originally Vietnam. [Comment on the blog post 'Weeknight ginger chicken pho ga (Vietnamese chicken soup)']. *Half Baked Harvest*. https://www.halfbakedharvest.com/chicken-pho/

Abidin, C., & Zeng, J. (2020). Feeling Asian together: Coping with #COVIDRacism on Subtle Asian Traits. *Social Media + Society*, *6*(3), 1–5. 205630512094822–2056305120948223. 10.1177/2056305120948223

AliceK. (2013, August 21). Wow, so glad that I stumbled upon this site trying to look for steamed egg cake recipe. I love reading. [Commented posted on 'The real Chinese grandmas']. *Chinese Grandma*. https://chinesegrandma.com/2010/07/the-real-chinese-grandmas/

Alyea, R. (2011, August 11). A rainbow peanut butter pie for Mikey. *Sweetapolita*. https://sweetapolita.com/blogs/recipes/how-to-make-a-rainbow-peanut-butter-pie-for-mikey/

Ang, I. (1991). *Desperately seeking the audience*. Routledge. 10.4324/9780203133347

Bane, C. M. H., Cornish, M., Erspamer, N., & Kampman, L. (2010). Self-disclosure through weblogs and perceptions of online and "real-life" friendships among female bloggers. *Cyberpsychology, Behavior and Social Networking*, *13*(2), 131–139. 10.1089/cyber.2009.0174

Baym, N. K. (2015). Connect with your audience! The relational labor of connection. *The Communication Review*, *18*(1), 14–22. 10.1080/10714421.2015.996401

Bell, D. & Hollows, J. (2007). Mobile homes. *Space and Culture*, *10*(1), 22–39. 10.1177/1206331206296380

boyd, d. (2010). Social network sites as networked publics: Affordances, dynamics, and implications. In Z. Papacharissi (Ed.), *A Networked Self: Identity, Community and Culture on Social Network Sites* (pp. 39–58). Routledge.

Cairns, K., Johnston, J., & MacKendrick, N. (2013). Feeding the "organic child": Mothering through ethical consumption. *Journal of Consumer Culture*, *13*(2), 97–118. 10.1177/1469540513480162

Carie. (2013). Bummer! Your grocery store doesn't have Silk Pure Almond? It doesn't have carrageenan. [Comment on the blog post 'Homemade oat milk – easy, fast cheap.'] *Oh She Glows*. https://ohsheglows.com/2013/01/10/homemade-oat-milk-easy-fast-cheap/comment-page-1/#comment-288641

Chen McTernan, C. (2021, March 7). Life lately. *Two Red Bowls*. https://tworedbowls.com/2021/03/07/life-lately/

Chen McTernan, C. (2021, September 20). Rose & lychee snowskin mooncakes. *Two Red Bowls*. https://tworedbowls.com/2021/09/20/rose-lychee-snowskin-mooncakes/

Crawford, R. (1980). Healthism and the medicalization of everyday life. *International Journal of Health Services*, *10*(3), 365–388. 10.2190/3H2H-3XJN-3KAY-G9NY

Doan, T. (2020, March 20). Mini chocolate cake. *Wild Wild Whisk*. https://wildwildwhisk.com/mini-chocolate-cake/

Doreen. (2013, September 5). Hi there. Came across your website after a rather grey, soberly discussion with my colleague that as a Chinese working. [Comment on the blog post 'The real Chinese grandmas.']. *Chinese Grandma*. https://chinesegrandma.com/2010/07/the-real-chinese-grandmas/

Drummond, R. (2010, September 8). Ten important things about blogging. *The Pioneer Woman*. https://www.thepioneerwoman.com/ree-drummond-life/a5220/ten-important-things-ive-learned-about-blogging/

Duffy, B. E. (2017). *(Not) getting paid to do what you love: Gender, social media, and aspirational work*. Yale University Press.

Emily. (2021, March 9). 'Luke and Clara are getting so big!!! I enjoyed reading about your life update–I hope your pregnancy gets easier.' [Comment on blog post 'life lately']. *Two Red Bowls*. https://tworedbowls.com/2021/03/07/life-lately/

Gerard, T. (2021, February 10). Weeknight ginger chicken pho ga (Vietnamese chicken soup). *Half-Baked Harvest*. https://www.halfbakedharvest.com/chicken-pho/

Hunter, A. (2016). Monetizing the mommy: Mommy blogs and the audience commodity. *Information, Communication and Society*, *19*(9), 1306–1320.

Jourdie. (2014, May 4). As the proud granddaughter of an awesome Chinese grandma, this history and recognition actually made me tear up. Yay for. [Comment on the blog post 'The real Chinese grandmas']. *Chinese Grandma*. https://chinesegrandma.com/2010/07/the-real-chinese-grandmas/

Keller, J. (2012). Virtual feminisms: Girls' blogging communities, feminist activism, and participatory politics. *Information, Communication & Society*, *15*(3), 429–447. 10.1080/1369118X.2011.642890

Kim, D. (2021). Racialized beauty, visibility, and empowerment: Asian American women influencers on YouTube. *Information, Communication & Society*, *Vol.ahead-of-print*(ahead-of-print), 1–18. 10.1080/1369118X.2021.1994726

Kiyuu. (2011, October 11). Oh wow, your site is very inspiring; I came here via googling 'chinese oatmeal,' haha, I've got to try some [Comment on the blog post 'The real Chinese grandmas']. *Chinese Grandma*. https://chinesegrandma.com/2010/07/the-real-chinese-grandmas/

Klaine. (2013). Hello, I have made many meals and desserts from your recipes. They were all delicious. Anyway, I would like to point [Comment on the blog post 'Homemade oat milk – easy, fast cheap.'] *Oh She Glows*. https://ohsheglows.com/2013/01/10/homemade-oat-milk-easy-fast-cheap/comment-page-1/#comment-293205

Leonardi, S. (1989). Recipes for reading: Summer pasta, lobster à la riseholme, and key lime pie. *PMLA: Publications of the Modern Language Association of America*, *104*(3), 340–347. 10.2307/462443

Liddon, A. (2013, January 10). Homemade oat milk – Easy, fast, cheap. *Oh She Glows*. https://ohsheglows.com/2013/01/10/homemade-oat-milk-easy-fast-cheap/

Lillian. (2010, July 26). The real Chinese grandmas. *Chinese Grandma.* https://chinesegrandma.com/2010/07/the-real-chinese-grandmas/

Liu, B. (2018, May 9). Scallion sambal milk bread. *Betty Liu.* https://bettysliu.com/2018/05/09/scallion-sambal-milk-bread/

Liu, B. (2019, January 29). Black sesame karaage. *Betty Liu.* https://bettysliu.com/2019/01/29/black-sesame-karaage/

Lopez, L. K. (2009). The radical act of "mommy blogging": redefining motherhood through the blogosphere. *New Media & Society, 11*(5), 729–747. 10.1177/1461444809105349

Lopez, L. K. (2014). Blogging while angry: the sustainability of emotional labor in the Asian American blogosphere. *Media, Culture & Society, 36*(4), 421–436. 10.1177/0163443714523808

Lynch, M. (2010). Healthy habits or damaging diets: An exploratory study of a food blogging community. *Ecology of Food and Nutrition, 49*(4), 316–335. 10.1080/03670244.2010.491054

Makinen, K. (2021). Resilience and vulnerability: Emotional and affective labour in mom blogging. *New Media & Society, 23*(10), 2964–2978. 10.1177/1461444820941196

Marwick, A. E. (2013). "They're really profound women, they're entrepreneurs": Conceptions of authenticity in fashion blogging. *Proceedings of the International Conference on Weblogs and Social Media (ICWSM).* http://www.tiara.org/wp-content/uploads/2018/05/amarwick_fashionblogs_ICWSM_2013.pdf

Marwick, A. E., & boyd, d. (2011). I tweet honestly, I tweet passionately: Twitter users, context collapse, and the imagined audience. *New Media & Society, 13*(1), 114–133. 10.1177/1461444810365313

Matchar, E. (2013). *Homeward bound: Why women are embracing the new domesticity.* Simon & Schuster.

McFeely, M. D. (2001). *Can she bake a cherry pie?: American women and the kitchen in the twentieth century.* University of Massachusetts Press.

McRobbie, A. (2016). *Be creative: Making a living in the new culture industries.* Polity Press.

Nikki. (2013). I don't like to promote Silk since it's owned by Dean Foods, but their almond milk IS non-gmo. [Comment on the blog post 'Homemade oat milk – easy, fast cheap.'] *Oh She Glows.* https://ohsheglows.com/2013/01/10/homemade-oat-milk-easy-fast-cheap/comment-page-1/#comment-321046

Ostrom, L. (2017, January 26). There you are: Afton's story, Part one. *Pinch of Yum.* https://pinchofyum.com/aftons-story-1

Parker, D., & Song, M. (2006). New ethnicities online: Reflexive racialisation and the internet. *The Sociological Review, 54*(3), 575–594. 10.1111/j.1467-954X.2006.00630.x

Perelman, D. (2016, November 10). Root vegetable gratin. *Smitten Kitchen.* https://smittenkitchen.com/2016/11/root-vegetable-gratin/

Perillo, J. (2011, August 14). 5:52pm. *In Jennie's Kitchen.* https://www.injennieskitchen.com/2011/08/552-pm-jennifer-perillo/

Ryan, M. E. (2018). *Lifestyle media in American culture: Gender, class, and the politics of ordinariness*. Routledge.

Sarah. (2013). Hi, We don't like carrageenan and fillers, so we use Rice Dream milk and love it! We buy the large [Comment on the blog post 'Homemade oat milk – easy, fast cheap.'] *Oh She Glows*. https://ohsheglows.com/2013/01/10/homemade-oat-milk-easy-fast-cheap/comment-page-1/#comment-369051

Suuronen, A., Reinikainen, H., Borchers, N. S., & Strandberg, K. (2021). When social media influencers go political: An exploratory analysis on the emergence of political topics among Finnish influencers. *Javnost – The Public, 29*(3), 301–317. 10.1080/13183222.2021.1983367

Tye, D. (2010). *Baking as biography: A life in recipes*. McGill-Queens University Press.

Tu, L. (2021, April 23). Pho: The humble soup that cause an outrage. *BBC Travel*. https://www.bbc.com/travel/article/20210421-pho-the-humble-soup-that-caused-an-outrage#:~:text=While%20most%20historians%20agree%20that,phonetic%20similarity%20to%20%22ph%E1%BB%9F%22.

Van Driel, L., & Dumitrica, D. (2021). Selling brands while staying "authentic": The professionalization of Instagram influencers. *Convergence, 27*(1), 66–84. 10.1177/1354856520902136

Vicky. (2014). Hi Sarah, I'm sorry to tell you research now indicates rice milk contains huge amounts of arsenic (yes, the poison!) [Comment on the blog post 'Homemade oat milk – easy, fast cheap.'] *Oh She Glows*. https://ohsheglows.com/2013/01/10/homemade-oat-milk-easy-fast-cheap/comment-page-1/#comment-570984

Wizenberg, M. (2016, November 30). November 30. *Orangette*. http://orangette.net/2016/11/november-30/

Yandell, K. (2011, August 13). Mikey's peanut butter pie. *The Meaning of Pie*. http://www.themeaningofpie.com/2011/08/mikeys-peanut-butter-pie/

4 #BlackoutTuesday and Influencer Activism on Instagram

#ImmigrantFoodStories was a networked action originating in the food blogosphere in February 2017 by Kimberley Hasselbrink in response to Trump's Executive Order 13769, commonly referred to as the "Muslim ban," which imposed a ban on people travelling to the United States on passports from Iran, Iraq, Libya, Somalia, Sudan, Syria, and Yemen. #ImmigrantFoodStories invited food bloggers to post a recipe with their families' and friends' immigration stories, which were cross-posted on participants' blogs as well as on a dedicated Instagram account. Food blogger Karen Chan of *Honestly Yum* posted a recipe for soy eggs with an explanation as to why she felt compelled to participate in this action:

> Yes, this post is political, but the events that have unfolded in the past two weeks cut beyond politics to a deeply personal level. I have the same story as many other people in this country: I am the daughter of two immigrant parents, who came to this country for a better life and sacrificed everything they had so that my sister and I could have every opportunity to become the people we wanted to be. My mother and grandmother were refugees that narrowly escaped a government regime that would have put them in a labor camp or worse.
>
> (2017)

Jenny Huang of *Hello My Dumpling* wrote about her parents' immigration story, noting that

> This country was built upon the backs of immigrants. It is because of the generations of people hoping and dreaming that this country is the world power that it is now. We must not forget that. We must not allow the current state of the government make

DOI: 10.4324/9781003302278-4

us forget that it is only through the embracing of our differences that we can be stronger.

(2017)

While these posts and recipes were superficially indistinguishable from the personal narratives upon which food blog posts are founded, this hashtag and the stories it generated represented a subtle foray into politics that was clearly oriented toward publicizing and criticizing Trump's racist and discriminatory politics.

While a subtle form of protest, #ImmigrantFoodStories was part of a larger shift in the food blogosphere in the wake of the 2016 US Presidential election where the shock and grief felt by many at Trump's presidency found its way onto the posts of prominent food bloggers. Deb Perelman, of *Smitten Kitchen*, added a footnote to her first post-election recipe describing it as "a sad, rough week" (2016) while Joy Wilson of *Joy the Baker* wrote that she would "miss President Obama's grace and generosity of spirit as our leader" and posted a link to Obama's NPR exit interview (2017). Despite their polite and softened references to the election outcome, these small actions and statements were revolutionary in collectively challenging the longstanding notion that food bloggers purposefully cultivate the trivial and the frivolous while staying silent on political topics. It is of course erroneous to suggest that the food blogosphere has ever been truly apolitical, as many scholars have pointed out the lifestyle and feminist politics implicit in these digital self-representations and life narratives. However, in the wake of the 2016 US Presidential election, food bloggers began to venture more explicitly into commentary about institutional politics, social justice, and activism on their branded platforms.

These next two chapters explore how Asian American food bloggers have grappled with the call to use their extensive brand influence – built upon the commercialisation of followers and lifestyle content – in the service of explicit social justice activism, and the ways they negotiate some of the major tensions between aspirational lifestyle content and the imperatives of online activism. This chapter documents this shift through the specific focus on Asian American food bloggers' participation in #BlackOutTuesday on Instagram in June 2020. #BlackoutTuesday had high uptake among influencers and is particularly helpful for illuminating the strategies and means through which influencers began to incorporate activist messages within their platforms, against criticisms of "performative activism," the term used to describe the practice of non-marginalized groups "profess[ing] support and solidarity with a marginalized group in a way that either isn't helpful or that actively harms that group" (Phillips, 2020).

I explore #BlackoutTuesday participation by my sample with a primary focus on analyzing their branded Instagram accounts including posts, images, captions, hashtags and comments, and interpreting this data in conjunction with my continued readings of the corresponding food blogs of this sample. The vast majority of professional food bloggers have Instagram accounts that are attached to their food blog brands as social media become important sites for cross-promoting their blog work: the visual emphasis of Instagram is particularly suited to the publication and circulation of the lavish images for which food blogs are known, and the widespread popularity of Instagram makes it increasingly useful as a platform for self-promotion. More pressingly, attention to Instagram posts situated food bloggers' response within the larger conversation and action around #BlackoutTuesday and Black Lives Matter which was largely centered on the Instagram platform. Asian American food bloggers demonstrated self-reflexivity through their posts, advocating thoughtfully and sincerely for action and education around racism in the United States, particularly around Black Lives Matter and the issue of police brutality. However, many of these posts and their recommended actions continued to rely on the logics of neoliberal individualism and consumer politics, and were primarily focused on activism that was contained within the food blogosphere and digital attention economy. Additionally, while Asian American bloggers drew upon their racial identities to demonstrate allyship with Black Americans and the Black Lives Matter movement, they simultaneously used distancing mechanisms that tended to perpetuate the model minority myth. These findings are indicative of the ongoing tensions that must be negotiated in the development of influencer activism in the Asian American food blogosphere.

The Changing Taste for Race-Based Activism

The new politicisation of the food blogosphere in 2016 is embedded within wider cultural changes where the shock of Trump's election led to much soul searching among well-educated, middle-class liberals (who are disproportionately represented as bloggers and readers of the food blogosphere) as a moment that solidified the grave ramifications of complacency or political silence on controversial issues. For instance, the emotional response to this election inspired millions of people to join the Women's March on Washington which, in its first iteration in 2017, was timed to take place on Trump's first full day in office and attracted a broad coalition of protesters to join satellite marches across the United States and the world. This new and positive attention to "popular feminism" (Banet-Weiser, 2018) had its roots in the growing trend toward the visibility of feminism which feminist media scholars noted had, since around 2014, begun to be recirculated as a hip and youth-driven identity (Banet-Weiser, 2015; Hamad & Taylor, 2015; Keller & Ryan, 2018). Additionally, while Black Lives Matter was founded by Alicia Garza, Patrisse Cullors and Opal Tometi in 2013 following the murder of Trayvon Martin, the momentum of this social movement increased exponentially after George Floyd's murder at the hands of police in Minnesota in May 2020. While Black Lives Matter had been growing steadily since its inception, Floyd's murder triggered protests of an unprecedented scale across the United States, with polls suggesting between 15–26 million Americans participated in protests at some point (Buchanan et al., 2020). The numbers of protesters at these two mass events can be taken as a measure of the resurgence in attention to activism and identity politics in the contemporary period.

The mainstream attention to structural racism in the wake of George Floyd's murder had ripple effects on food media culture as the overarching whiteness and privilege of foodie culture (Johnston & Baumann, 2010) was interrogated through a series of high-profile racial controversies. In early June 2020, Adam Rappaport, then the chief editor of flagship food magazine *Bon Appetit*, resigned after photos of him adopting brown face for Halloween in 2004 surfaced and ignited allegations about the mistreatment of employees of color and problematic presentation of food from different cultures at the magazine (Severson, 2020b). Alison Roman, a white food writer and columnist for the *New York Times*, publicly criticized the work and success of celebrity entrepreneurs of color Marie Kondo and Chrissy Teigen, igniting public backlash and highlighting Roman's history of culinary cultural appropriation (Saxena, 2020). Additionally, John T. Edge, the white director of the Southern Foodways Alliance since 1999, faced increasing pressure to resign to afford the opportunity for a person of color to head the influential Alliance and to encourage more diversity within the organization (Severson, 2020a). *Thug Kitchen*, a blog by two white content creators that since 2012 had unapologetically defended their brand's reliance on racist African American stereotypes and vernacular, finally changed their blog's name with a message that: "whatever our original intention, our use of the term ['thug'] reflected our privilege and ignored the reality that the word is assigned to black people in an attempt to dehumanize them" (Bad Manners, 2020). The cumulative effect of these events was to signal a growing pressure to acknowledge and respond to structural racism in foodie culture and food media.

Many food bloggers were inspired to respond to this moment through their eager participation in #BlackoutTuesday, a social media action devised by Black music executives Brianna Agyemang and Jamila Thomas as a call for the music industry to pause and reflect on their participation in structural racism (an affiliate hashtag used was #TheShowMustBePaused) (Donoughue, 2020). As the Instagram action grew in June 2020 – aided through posts by celebrities including Rihanna, Taylor Swift, and Billie Eilish – it was popularly represented through posting a black square which symbolized muting the aspirational and commercialized content prevalent on Instagram in favor of showcasing Black voices and resources on the Black Lives Matter movement and activism. The majority of Saveur-nominated food bloggers engaged with Black Lives Matter content in some form during June 2020 and the months following. Yet, given the widespread uptake of #BlackoutTuesday among non-Black celebrities and influencers, participation was often viewed with some skepticism. "Performative activism" and "optical allyship" were terms commonly used to denote influencers taking advantage of or seeking to profit from the "opportunities" presented by protests, epitomized by widely-shared footage of influencer Fiona Moriarty-McLaughlin who was photographed pretending to board up a looted storefront in Santa Monica before immediately driving away in a luxury vehicle. Many influencers were also implored, often publicly through the comments, to remove the #BlackLivesMatter hashtag to avoid crowding out vital posts about protests and the movement and these comments functioned as an implicit critique of influencers' ill-considered and non-vital contributions to this movement. This critique also reinforced a boundary between "legitimate" activism and influencer labor, which has often been stereotyped as self-serving, entrepreneurial, shallow, and narcissistic. These competing and controversial discourses set the scene for Asian American food bloggers' participation in #BlackoutTuesday on Instagram.

Racial Activism as Brand Strategy

#BlackoutTuesday signaled a tipping point across the food blogosphere where bloggers were compelled to use their digital influence to advocate for political and social issues. As Michelle Tam indignantly begins her post, "No, I'm not going to stick to food" (2020a) and this sentiment was evidenced through the large numbers of bloggers who declared their need to speak up or their guilt about not having previously used their digital platforms to support social justice issues. This integration of activist dialogue within food bloggers' pre-existing branded content required negotiation of the inherent tensions between activist messages and aspirational lifestyle content, for while activism has long been practiced in and through commercial markets (Banet-Weiser, 2012; Cohen, 2003), the tone of the food blogosphere has generally worked to silence politicized – and what some consider controversial – topics such as the state-sanctioned murder of Black Americans. While Asian American food bloggers' participation in #BlackoutTuesday could be characterized as earnest and action-oriented, and this action marked a significant tonal shift in the apoliticism typically embraced in this digital culture (Lofgren, 2013), there was still a focus on folding this content into – rather than disrupting – the branded food content around which blogger's Instagram accounts were based. This generated social justice dialogue that was contained within the logics of postrace and postfeminism, for instance through simplifying the issue to one of Black representation in digital food media or the framing of social justice action as a project of neoliberal individual responsibility.

Many Asian American food bloggers drew on techniques of creative entrepreneurialism to smoothly integrate Black Lives Matter content into their digital food brands. For instance, while #BlackoutTuesday was popularly represented through posting black squares on Instagram, several food bloggers opted to post food or cooking images that were symbolically aligned with the theme of racial justice and activism. These included an image of black-and-white cookies, a sugar cookie iced with the phrase "we cannot stay silent about things that actually matter," and an image of cake batter with the word "muted" posted across it. These images allowed activist content to be inserted into food bloggers' Instagram accounts while maintaining visual consistency with the existing branded content. Similarly, many food bloggers promoted actions to support the businesses, brands and creative work of people of color through featuring recipes and books by Black cooks and chefs, tagging the accounts of Black foodies and food bloggers, and promoting Black-owned food businesses. For instance, Michelle Tam (2020b) of *Nom Nom Paleo* features an image of a recipe by Black blogger @confessionsofacleaneater while oyster sommelier Julie Qiu of *In a Half Shell* posts a list of BIPOC oyster and seafood professionals to follow (2020b). Additionally, several bloggers actively channel their racial justice activism through the entrepreneurial pathways set up through their food blogs. Some food bloggers reference the social justice action they wished to take within their own brands, drawing on the language of corporate philanthropy, as Terri and Jenny of *Spoon, Fork, Bacon* write, "We will also be making a point of including more Black and POC owned businesses, and authors in our content. There are a lot of talented amazing Black and POC food bloggers and chefs that we don't know, and we should" (Spoonforkbacon, 2020).

These images and posts distil the problem to Black representation in digital food media as a way of seamlessly integrating Black Lives Matter messaging into their branded lifestyle content. However, this myopic framing momentarily amplifies Black creatives' content while failing to interrogate the structural racism implicit within the attention economy and food blogosphere, provoking Black food blogger Angela Davis of *Kitchenista* to write:

> I see those of you who have blacked out and muted but those comments are turned off. It's cowardly, to say the least. The very least you can do is directly deal with the racist comments your own audiences spew. Deal with that before you tag me as your black blogger of the week for performative activism.
>
> (2020)

That is, the expression of #BlackoutTuesday as a process of content amplification and muting was impossible to understand outside of a calculated brand strategy where the cost of not participating in this highly visible action had to be measured against the potential loss of followers or, in other words, material impacts on the blogger's business. Moreover, this framing of the issue within food media culture suggests that Asian American food bloggers' authority to speak on this issue is based on their *expertise* as food bloggers, rather than their *experience* as non-white Americans who have firsthand knowledge of the impacts of structural racism. While sharing personal experience, or the "personalization of politics" often characterizes the input of activists participating in large contemporary hashtag activist movements such as #MeToo and #BlackLivesMatter (Bennett, 2012; Jackson et al., 2020) – food bloggers' reliance on their expertise as justification for participating in fact limited their commentary to the world of food media, and continued the self-censorship of personal experiences of racism by Asian American food bloggers. That is, many Asian American food bloggers were, in fact, sticking to food in favor of using this moment to discuss more personal experiences of race and racism.

Of course, food bloggers also advocated for their followers to support broader social organisations and NGOs that were directed toward materially supporting the Black Lives Matter movement, urging their readers to act through pledging donations for and signing petitions created by various activist organizations. For example, Michelle Lopez of *Hummingbird High* sets up a donation matching fundraiser with her followers. She writes: "I spent the week matching donations for black-owned and black-led social justice organizations ... Together, we raised almost $6k for the different causes!" (2020). Another popular action included sharing educational content and resources. For instance, Andrea Nguyen (2020) of *Viet World Kitchen* posts a link to a *Washington Post* article covering the protests while Michelle Tam of *Nom Nom Paleo* posts a list of books for further reading about race (2020b). However, these popular calls to action tend to situate activism firmly within the sphere of neoliberal individual responsibility. The imperative to self-educate about racism aligned well with the networks for formal and informal knowledge exchange established by the food blogging community but could easily be reduced to a project of white moral virtue whose ultimate goal stops at self-knowledge rather than engaging in sustained and collective political activism. Similarly, calls to donate money demonstrated an overreliance on consumer activism and the free market as a way of impacting structural social change, continuing a theme of consumer choice and empowerment that has long been entrenched in the alternative food movement (Guthman, 2011).

Finally, while this conversation demonstrated a desire to connect dialogue in the food blogosphere to timely social justice events, conversation was also contained through the use of platforms and temporality. It should be noted that while the majority of food bloggers made some reference to #BlackoutTuesday or Black Lives Matter on Instagram, very few posted additional content on their food blogs themselves. This allowed food bloggers to signal participation in networked Instagram conversation on Black Lives Matter while also preserving the illusion of their food blogs – through which the majority of sponsored partnerships and content takes place – as largely free of overt or explicit political discussion, commentary, or controversy. Additionally, several food bloggers also ultimately deleted their Instagram posts on Black Lives Matter for unknown reasons. These posts were also limited in their temporality. Many food bloggers acknowledged that Black Lives Matter posts were being inserted into what would continue as a food media account, framing these discussions as a pause or temporary diversion in food content, as several bloggers reassured their readers that they would "get back to posting about food soon." While many food bloggers presented ongoing posts about the movement and activism on Instagram, these posts never continued beyond a month or so after the initial outpouring generated by Black Out

Tuesday. That is, despite many pledges and commitments that this action would contribute to longstanding change, it rarely made sense for food blog brands to continue the specific focus on and attention to Black Lives Matter and structural racism on these platforms outside of the moment authorized through the #BlackoutTuesday action. This inbuilt obsolescence had the effect of making conversation visible as a fleeting trend, which is exactly what many critics of this action had predicted.

Taken together, these features of food bloggers' participation in #BlackoutTuesday challenged the notion that food blogs are intentionally devoid of discourse on controversial social issues and institutional politics. However, these social justice contributions were nevertheless bound by the logics of the food blog as a brand and they tended to reinforce solutions to social issues that were individualized and entrepreneurial, which fit in particularly well with neoliberal and consumer-based understandings of social justice without necessarily committing to sustained social change nor actions that inherently pose any challenge to structural racism. This analysis is not intended as criticism of individual food bloggers – as I have argued, participation could be characterized as eager and earnest, and bloggers demonstrated creativity in enfolding activism into their brands – but it is indicative of the continued limits to using the heavily branded space of the food blogosphere to disseminate social justice messages.

Rhetorical Distancing and the Model Minority Myth

Asian American food bloggers occupied a unique space within #BlackoutTuesday conversation, given their status as a racial minority within the predominantly white food blogosphere and a community of color who were not the focus of the Black Lives Matter movement, a positioning that can be understood through racial triangulation theory. Claire Kim theorizes that Asian Americans are "racially triangulated" from white and Black Americans in the United States in a field of racial positions that "emphasizes both that groups become racialized in comparison with one another and that they are differently racialized" (1999, p. 107). Within this racial field, Asian Americans are subjected to the dual processes of

> 'relative valorization,' whereby dominant group A (Whites) valorizes subordinate group B (Asian American) relative to subordinate group C (Blacks) on cultural and/or racial grounds in order to dominate both groups, but especially the latter, and ... 'civic ostracism,' whereby dominant group A (Whites) constructs

subordinate group B (Asian Americans) as immutably foreign and unassimilable with Whites on cultural and/or racial grounds in order to ostracize them from the body politic and civic membership.

(Kim, 1999, p. 107)

This first process of "relative valorization" corresponds to myths of Asian American exceptionalism and cultural narratives that Asian Americans are highly-educated, affluent and assimilated within – and privy to the privileges of – white culture. The danger of the model minority myth, however, is that it fails to take into account Asian Americans' continued precarity through their "civic ostracism" which has the potential to oppress and exclude Asian Americans at the whims and varying political agendas of white supremacy. Moreover, adhering to the model minority myth works to perpetuate historical divisions sowed between Asian American and Black American communities. The discussion of race in the #BlackoutTuesday posts of Asian American food bloggers demonstrates an internalization of this subject positioning and the model minority myth.

Across Instagram, many food bloggers were open about the discomfort and hesitation they felt in talking about race and framed this as a hurdle that they had to overcome for the moral good. As Trang Doan of *Wild Wild Whisk* writes,

> Talking about food is easy, talking about your feelings, your believes [sic], your views of the world is difficult. I couldn't even type this without stopping multiple times looking for the right words. There are no right words, these are just my words.
>
> (2020)

As previously discussed, Asian American food bloggers overwhelmingly relied on their expertise as food bloggers, rather than their experience of race and racism as Asian Americans, to participate in this online conversation. This hesitation and uncertainty around discussing race in terms other than commodification, which is a feature of the postrace discourse of food blogs, is further characterized by distancing strategies that Asian American bloggers used to rhetorically distance their experiences of race and racism from those of Black Americans.

Many Asian American food bloggers maintained a purposeful sense of distance in relation to their racialized experience and that of Black Americans. This was often explained through acknowledging their privileges – for instance, as Doan writes, "I'm not white but I also feel privileged because of the opportunities I have been given" (2020). Without denying this self-expression of privilege, and the importance for non-Black allies to acknowledge such privilege, while Asian American food bloggers do tend to derive from more privileged socioeconomic backgrounds this fact might be more accurately attributed to their status as professional food bloggers – given the cultural capital, skills and resources currently required to maintain a quality food blog – than to their racial backgrounds. In acknowledging privilege in conjunction with their racial identity, Asian American food bloggers perpetuate the model minority myth by contributing to the erasure of heterogeneity and the socioeconomic bifurcation within the Asian American community. A further way in which Asian American food bloggers distinguished their experiences from those of Black Americans was through briefly discussing the racism they had experienced but qualifying it as not as serious, pervasive, or violent. For instance, Hannah Dela Cruz of *Make It Dough* identifies as a person of color and acknowledges that her racial background is the basis of her allyship through the shared experience of racism while also making clear that her experience of microaggressions were not to be confused with the fatal violence experienced by Black Americans as she writes:

> These are the hands of the POC, Filipinx immigrant who creates all of the bread you see on this channel. I have experienced countless racist microaggressions, but I have never, and perhaps will never experience the racist macro aggressions that black and brown people do. Still I see their struggle and I stand with them. As a POC I enjoy my rights as a free American because of the civil disobedience of the Black Panthers and Civil Rights Activists and I know that the reforms that the #BlackLivesMatter Movement is fighting for will benefit ALL OF US (2020).

This rhetorical distancing and minimizing of the racism experienced by Asian Americans might be interpreted as a mark of respect given the significance of Black Lives Matter as a movement that arises from the specific history and experiences of Black Americans and that has solidified in the past decade through mourning the many deaths of Black men and women in the United States. In recognition of this fact, the terms BIPOC and "people of color" were often avoided as they were considered to detract from the movement's purposeful focus on the state's disproportionate impact on Black Americans (Kim, 2020). However, perpetuating the model minority myth denies the continuing precarity for all Asian Americans within Western settler colonialism –

a precarity that can swiftly turn to fatal violence against Asian Americans, as became evident in the wake of the covid-19 pandemic.

For this reason, rather than outlining the individual harms they had or had not experienced as a result of structural racism it was generally more productive for Asian American food bloggers to draw on their racial identities as the basis for their allyship with Black Americans. They did so through purposefully adopting the political identity term "Asian American" – and in doing so invoking the 1960s historical and activist roots of this term which was inspired in part by the Black power movement (Hsu, 2019) – which deviates from the racial qualifiers that indicate racial commodification on food blogs, such as "Korean," "fusion," "pan-Asian," and "Asian-inspired." Moreover, these political identity terms are drawn upon specifically to interpellate the Asian American community and compel them to act in support of Black Lives Matter. For instance, Doan writes that she wishes to share resources on "how the Asian and Asian American community can show up for our Black friends during this time" (2020) while several food bloggers employ the hashtags #YellowPerilforBlackPower and #AsiansforBlackLives to signal a similar sentiment. Yet, it is worth noting that the hashtag #YellowPerilforBlackPower – which circulated on Instagram due to its association with a popular and striking piece of art by Monyee Chau through her Instagram account @monyeeart – was similarly controversial, with debates on the value and sensitivity of using or reclaiming the terms "yellow" and "yellow peril," and the appropriateness of focusing on Asian American struggles during the 2020 wave of Black Lives Matter protests (Kim, 2020; Littaua, 2020; Weik, 2020). As Chau writes in a widely-shared Instagram album attached to her iconic artwork:

> Gratitude to folks who are calling me in and reminding me that this is not a time to center Asian struggle. I want Asians to remember that bottom line, we are here to protect our Black sisters, brothers, siblings. Because Black Lives Matter. We are here to reject this narrative of being a model minority and stand in solidarity
>
> (2020)

Despite the differing perspectives on this issue, these posts and comment spaces demonstrate how participation in this action comprised a productive process of debate and understanding – grappling both with learning more about the best ways to demonstrate allyship with the Black Lives Matter movement and to challenge the model minority myth – that is negotiated through posts, edits and comments. As blogger Qiu writes, in an amendment to her original #BlackoutTuesday post that demonstrates the potential feedback loop between bloggers, activists and readers:

> It is not my intention to offend or come off as unsympathetic to the injustices that black people face with this post. I understand now having received some of your critiques that it reads differently. I am learning as I go and would much rather have a conversation about the issues, and explore my own subconscious prejudices than not (2020a).

Conclusion

In a widely-shared Instagram story (later preserved as an Instagram post), Jenny Huang of *Hello My Dumpling* – who, since food blogging, has forged a successful career as a food photographer – talks about the dilution and colonization of ethnic food through the structural processes of the inherently white food media industry. She writes,

> As POC in food media … time and time again, we find our stories ignored, our recipes and ingredients appropriated, and our voice stolen … We need to be able to tell our own stories. We don't need your telling it for us.
>
> (2020)

Huang's commentary was written in response to Adam Rappaport's brownface controversy and points out the continued marginalization of people of color in the food industry. However, as this chapter also demonstrates, the ability for Asian American food bloggers to "tell [their] own stories" is also subject to negotiation within the food blogging platform and community, which constrains their voices and shapes the racialized narratives they are able to tell on and through their own digital platforms.

Asian American food bloggers' participation in #BlackoutTuesday was thoughtful and demonstrated a sincere intent to use their platforms to enact social justice while performing allyship with Black Americans. At the same time, there were continued constraints on Asian Americans food bloggers' discussion of race and racism through this digital action. In particular, very few food bloggers were able to draw on their personal experiences of racism and tended to rhetorically fuel the model minority myth. Additionally, activism was generally contained to actions that could be performed within food and social media circles, as well as in line with the ethos of neoliberal individualism and consumer choice. Rather than presenting these facts as failures of these food bloggers, they might be understood as evidence of the continuing ways in which internalization of the model minority myth, platforms and the digital culture of the food blogosphere work to silence and decenter the racial identities and experiences of Asian American food bloggers.

Moreover, even though participating in #BlackoutTuesday was dictated by a community of food bloggers on Instagram, individual bloggers often continue to bear the brunt of criticism and emotional labor as a result of their participation. Specific to the discussion of race through such action, Asian American food bloggers attracted a cacophony of extreme opinions on their #BlackoutTuesday posts, some of which is recorded through the comments displayed on these posts. Bloggers are criticized from both ends of the spectrum – they are mocked for their posts which are viewed as trend-chasing and superficial shows of activism or support and they are criticized by bigoted audience members who propose that the Black Lives Matter movement is racist and demand to know why bloggers do not support Blue Lives Matter and All Lives Matter. Bloggers are angrily chided by readers exasperated by the insertion of "politics" into their food blog feeds and threatened with unfollows; yet, they also receive much support from readers who post hearts and affirm Black Lives Matter content, and thank them for speaking up and using their platforms. Some comments air the opinions and propaganda of racists in the community, ultimately giving denigrators of the Black Lives Matter movement seemingly equal voice and potentially legitimizing their racist opinions on this matter, which enacts further trauma on minority readers and followers as well as on Asian American food bloggers whose accounts host this racism. These responses are intended to emphasize my suggestion that food bloggers' participation in Blackout Tuesday cannot simply be dismissed as trend-chasing but involves acknowledging the emotional labor demanded of food bloggers and the heightened vulnerability of Asian American food bloggers in this community.

Despite these limitations and the ambivalent ways in which racial discourses were presented through this action, it is clear that #BlackoutTuesday marked a moment of significance within the blogosphere as activism was explicitly embraced as a topic to be circulated through the networks of influence built up by individual food bloggers. This shift in the conventions of the food blogosphere demonstrates the malleability of this digital culture, which arises from the collective and networked labors of individual bloggers. What is promising is not the critical performance of race, but the receptiveness to change and dialogue which is supported by the food blogging community. In the next chapter, I explore how these responses and reflections on racism come to light through the #StopAsianHate movement and events which more specifically underlined the gravity and fatal consequences of continued structural racism for the Asian American community.

References

Bad Manners. (2020). We're Changing. *Bad Manners.* https://www.badmanners.com/change

Banet-Weiser, S. (2012). *AuthenticTM: The politics of ambivalence in a brand culture.* New York University Press.

Banet-Weiser, S. (2015, January 21). Popular misogyny: A zeitgeist. *Culture Digitally.* https://culturedigitally.org/2015/01/popular-misogyny-a-zeitgeist/

Banet-Weiser, S. (2018). *Empowered: Popular feminism and popular misogyny.* Duke University Press.

Bennett, W. L. (2012). The personalization of politics: Political identity, social media, and changing patterns in participation. *The American Academy of Political and Social Science, 664*(1), 20–39.

Buchanan, L., Bui, Q., & Patel, J. K. (2020, July 3). Black Lives Matter may be the largest movement in U.S. history. *The New York Times.* https://www.nytimes.com/interactive/2020/07/03/us/george-floyd-protests-crowd-size.html

Chan, K. (2017, February 7). Lu dan (soy eggs). *Honestly Yum.* https://honestlyyum.com/18507/

Chau, M. [@monyeeart]. (2020, June 6). Really important conversation about Yellow Peril supports Black Power! Let us practice this routine of unlearning our internalized oppression. I. [Album]. *Instagram.* https://www.instagram.com/p/CBEHSsPJNuP/

Cohen, L. (2003). *A consumers' republic: The politics of mass consumption in postwar America.* Alfred A. Knopf.

Davis, A. [@thekitchenista]. (2020, June 3). You already know. #blackouttuesday. Returning to edit this to say – I see those of you who have blacked out and [Photograph]. *Instagram.* https://www.instagram.com/p/CA784DFpl-9/

Dela Cruz, H. [@makeitdough]. (2020, June 2). I turned to sourdough as a form of escapism, and I know you guys are following me for the same reason. [Photograph]. *Instagram.* https://www.instagram.com/p/CA6eZiGpTr2/

Doan, T. [@wildwildwhisk]. (2020, June 2). Talking about food is easy, talking about your feelings, your believes, your views of the world is difficult. I couldn't [Photograph]. *Instagram.* https://www.instagram.com/p/CA7vCVdFbdt/

Donoughue, P. (2020, June 3). What the #BlackoutTuesday movement means and why it has turned your Instagram dark. *ABC News.* https://www.abc.net.au/news/2020-06-03/instagram-went-dark-for-black-out-tuesday-heres-why/12315146

Guthman, J. (2011). *Weighing in: Obesity, food justice, and the limits of capitalism*. University of California Press. 10.1525/9780520949751

Hamad, H., & Taylor, A. (2015). Introduction: Feminism and contemporary celebrity culture. *Celebrity Studies, 6*(1), 124–127. 10.1080/19392397.2015.100538

Hsu, H. (2019, December 30). The Asian-American canon breakers. *The New Yorker.* https://www.newyorker.com/magazine/2020/01/06/the-asian-american-canon-breakers

Huang, J. (2017, February 9). My Sichuan. A country of immigrants. Sichuan beer braised duck with mushrooms + daikon. *Hello My Dumpling.* http://www.hellomydumpling.com/sichuan-beer-braised-duck-mushrooms-daikon/

Huang, J. [@hellomydumpling]. (2020, June 10). Posting what I wrote in my stories yesterday here so it doesn't disappear. I have been hearing from so many. *Instagram.* https://www.instagram.com/p/CBOxqW_jyPT/

Jackson, S. J., Bailey, M., & Foucault Welles, B. (2020). *#Hashtag activism: Networks of race and gender justice*. MIT Press.

Johnston, J., & Baumann, S. (2010). *Foodies: Democracy and distinction in the gourmet foodscape*. Routledge.

Keller, J., & Ryan, M. E. (2018). *Emergent feminisms: Complicating a postfeminist media culture*. Routledge.

Kim, E. T. (2020, July 29). The perils of "people of color". *The New Yorker.* https://www.newyorker.com/news/annals-of-activism/the-perils-of-people-of-color

Kim, C. J. (1999). The racial triangulation of Asian Americans. *Politics & Society, 27*(1), 105–138. 10.1177/0032329299027001005

Littaua, J. (2020, June 18). 'Yellow peril supports Black power': Reclaiming the word 'yellow'. *Asia Media International.* https://asiamedia.lmu.edu/2020/06/18/yellow-peril-supports-black-power-reclaiming-the-word-yellow/

Lofgren, J. M. (2013). *Changing tastes in food media: A study of recipe sharing traditions in the food blogging community*. [Masters by Research thesis, Queensland University of Technology]. QUT ePrints.

Lopez, M. [@hummingbirdhigh]. (2020, June 9). THE WORK IS NOT OVER! In case you missed it, I spent the week matching donations for black-owned and [Photograph]. *Instagram.* https://www.instagram.com/p/CBLpzdcBuo2/

Nguyen, A. [@andreanguyen88]. (2020, June 2). "My father grew up under Bangladeshi dictatorship, and he had friends killed by police, so he knows what to do [Photograph]. *Instagram.* https://www.instagram.com/p/CA5aZaijaSD/

Perelman, D. (2016, November 10). Root vegetable gratin. *Smitten Kitchen.* https://smittenkitchen.com/2016/11/root-vegetable-gratin/

Phillips, H. (2020, May 10). Performative allyship is deadly (here's what to do instead). *Medium.* https://forge.medium.com/performative-allyship-is-deadly-c900645d9f1f

Qiu, J. [@inahalfshellblog]. (2020a, May 29). I came across this remarkable quote by author Zora Neale Hurston years ago, but was waiting for the right moment to [Photograph]. *Instagram.* https://www.instagram.com/p/CAwZsUyJamw/

Qiu, J. [@inahalfshellblog]. (2020b, June 2020). Oyster 101: Five Black Oyster Pros to KnowThe first series of what I hope will be many to come [Photograph]. https://www.instagram.com/p/CBomqK-BIl6/

Saxena, J. (2020, May 11). What exactly is going on between Chrissy Teigen and Alison Roman on Twitter? *Eater.* https://www.eater.com/2020/5/11/21254554/chrissy-teigen-alison-roman-twitter-fallout-explained

Severson, K. (2020a, July 1). A white gatekeeper of Southern food faces calls to resign. *The New York Times.* https://www.nytimes.com/2020/06/29/dining/john-t-edge-southern-foodways-alliance.html

Severson, K. (2020b, June 8). Bon Appétit Editor Adam Rapoport Resigns. *The New York Times.* https://www.nytimes.com/2020/06/08/dining/bon-appetit-adam-rapoport.html

Spoonforkbacon. [@spoonforkbacon]. (2020, June 9). We have been doing a lot of research and a lot of listening the past couple of days. We have [Photograph]. *Instagram.* https://www.instagram.com/p/CBLpqshpXR8/

Tam, M. [@NomNomPaleo] (2020b, May 31). No, I'm not going to stick to food. It's past time to educate ourselves and our kids, listen with empathy [Photograph]. *Instagram.* https://www.instagram.com/p/CA03HnxDWG6/

Tam, M. [@NomNomPaleo] (2020a, June 4). You know a simple & tasty way to support a Black business owner? Go visit a food blog run by a Black [Photograph]. *Instagram.* https://www.instagram.com/p/CA_pG-mjUII/

Weik, T. (2020, June 10). The history behind 'yellow peril supports Black Power' and why some find it problematic. *NBCNews.* https://www.nbcnews.com/news/asian-america/history-behind-yellow-peril-supports-black-power-why-some-find-n1228776

Wilson, J. (2017, January 15). Let it be Sunday, 102! Good grief. *Joy the Baker.* https://joythebaker.com/2017/01/let-it-be-sunday-102/

5 #StopAsianHate and Asian American Activism on Food Blogs

In the wake of the global covid-19 pandemic and its widespread social impacts, there was a marked rise in violent and abusive hate crimes directed towards Asian Americans. Many Asian Americans and the global Asian diaspora were subject to abuse due to racism originating from the connection between China and the origins of covid-19, undoubtedly fueled by Donald Trump's explicitly racist and purposefully incendiary language in describing covid-19 as the "China Flu" or "Kung Flu." In the United States, there were multiple instances of unprovoked violent and fatal attacks against Asian Americans including the murder of Vicha Ratanapakdee, an 84-year old Thai American man who was fatally shoved to the ground on the streets of San Francisco; Noel Quintana, a Filipino American man whose face was slashed with a box cutter on the New York subway; and, Xiao Zhen Xie, a 75-year old Asian American woman who was punched in San Francisco and achieved notoriety by hitting her attacker back with a wooden board. Stop AAPI Hate, an initiative set up in 2002 by AAPI Equity, Chinese for Affirmative Action, and the Asian American Studies Department of San Francisco State University, compiled statistics of self-reported attacks on Asian Americans in the wake of the pandemic and recorded nearly 3800 incidents including verbal and physical assaults in 2020; by the end of 2021 this number had risen to 10, 905 incidents (Yellow Horse et al., 2022).

Further attention to the threat of violence experienced by the Asian American community became a focus in mainstream media in March 2021 after a mass shooting in Atlanta where white gunman Robert Aaron Long murdered eight people at three massage parlors, including six women of Asian descent. In the coverage and prosecution of this mass murder there was a reluctance to identify this as a race-based hate crime, ignorantly circulating stereotypes about Asian American women and sex work while downplaying the racial motivations behind

DOI: 10.4324/9781003302278-5

this murder. Indeed, at a press conference on the shooting, Georgia sheriff's captain Jay Baker told reporters that "yesterday was a really bad day for [Long] and this is what he did" (Guardian Staff, 2021). Baker's offensive, gross minimization of these murders was exacerbated by revelations that he had previously "shared images on Facebook of T-shirts that contained a racist slogan about China and the coronavirus" (Guardian Staff, 2021). More insidiously, a general sentiment of ignorance was cultivated in the salacious description of the shooting as fuelled by Long's sex obsession, rather than acknowledging the significance of this murderous rampage as a race-based hate crime. This charged atmosphere of fear and violence against Asian Americans led to the rise of #StopAsianHate as a hashtag conversation and social movement, which was supported by protest marches that were held across the US, designed to draw attention to and rally against race-based violence towards Asian Americans and the global Asian diaspora.

In this chapter, I explore the growth of the Stop Asian Hate movement within the context of the pandemic and Atlanta shootings, and its contours as a contemporary Asian American activist movement. Building on the discussions of #BlackoutTuesday and influencer activism, I detail three examples of Asian American food blogs that incorporated #StopAsianHate dialogue within their branded food platforms, demonstrating the possibilities for deeper engagement with Asian identity politics through digital lifestyle brands. These examples inform some suggested guidelines for effective Asian American political advocacy within the visibility logics of the food blogosphere.

The Nascent #StopAsianHate Movement

The hashtag #StopAsianHate went viral on social media in early 2021, used to reference the increase in abuse and violent crime experienced by Asian Americans and then peaking exponentially in mid-March 2021 in the days following the mass shooting of six Asian American women in Atlanta, and physical #StopAsianHate protests in several locations across the United States in late March. Stopasianhate.info – a website described as "a work-in-progress space to centralize information and important links in support of the #StopAsianHate movement" (@joeynogood, n.d.) – posits three primary goals for this movement: "1. Read about the current crisis of anti-Asian hate and violence 2. Raise awareness by sharing information with the media and your circle 3. Commit to anti-racist action by volunteering at, donating to, and advocating for all marginalized people." (@joeynogood, n.d.).

These first two steps present #StopAsianHate primarily as an information campaign, directed towards dispelling the model minority myth by providing evidence of the ongoing discrimination and racial violence experienced by the Asian American community. The need for this information campaign is underlined by the failure of police and mainstream media to recognize the Atlanta shootings as a race-based hate crime, grim evidence of the extent to which violence against the Asian American community continues to be invisibilized and minimized. Prominent AAPI activists, including the founders of Stop AAPI Hate – Cynthia Choi, Manjusha Kulkarni, and Russell Jeung – further advocate for greater investment in AAPI education as a key goal of the movement and for improving the outcomes of Asian American communities as well as other communities of color (Choi et al., 2022). There is some evidence that this information campaign has been successful in raising awareness of the continued discrimination faced by the Asian American community. Citing a UCLA survey, Vox journalist Li Zhou (2022) claims that between 2017 and 2021 "the percentage of people who believed Asian Americans experienced significant discrimination more than doubled" and that, according to NBC News, Google searches for the term "Asian American" increased 5000% in 2021 (Zhou, 2022).

This focus on visibility politics links #StopAsianHate to the Black Lives Matter movement, although the specific ways in which visibility is politicized is distinct and based on the respective needs and racial politics of the Asian American and Black American communities. For instance, visibility in the Black Lives Matter movement was centered around the citizen journalism and networked evidence of police brutality that targeted the Black community (Jackson et al., 2020), and for some outside the community this video footage was central to underlining the nature and prevalence of this state-sanctioned violence and building this social justice movement. Similarly, the "say their names" campaign which circulates the names of Black individuals killed by law enforcement officers is an important form of visibility and protest that honours the memory and speaks to the number of fatalities arising from institutional racism and white supremacy (Say Their Names, n.d.), with intersectional feminist scholars focusing on emphasizing the names of Black women victims to address the sidelining and invisibilization of women within the Black Lives Matter movement (Crenshaw, 2016; Tynes, Shuschke & Noble, 2016). While the CCTV footage circulated of violent attacks, particularly against Asian American elders, was central to attracting mainstream media attention to the issue of the continued racism and discrimination enacted against the Asian American community, the visibility of this campaign appeared to be directed at least in part toward the Asian American community themselves. Some of the accompanying news reports that are bookmarked on the #StopAsianHate website are directed toward encouraging the Asian American community to overcome the preference for silence over activism, encouraging this community to be vocal and visible activists. For instance, in a *Medium* article by Diana Chow posted to the website, Chow writes how the model minority myth has conditioned her to "sit down and be quiet. Do the work, keep [her head down" (2021) as an explanation for the seeming lack of activism within the Asian American community in response to the events that triggered the Stop Asian Hate movement.

The third goal of the movement situates the struggle for Asian American equality within a broader fight against race-based oppression, articulated more explicitly on the website as solidarity with Black Americans: "To be actively anti-racist we must fight against anti-Blackness in AAPI communities and society as a whole" (@joeynogood, n.d.). This articulated commitment to solidarity with Black Americans addresses the ugly history of racial tensions between Black Americans and Asian Americans, again stoked by the model minority myth and which Anne Anlin Cheng (2021) argues has generated discomfort amongst some in the Asian American community who have felt reluctant to report street assaults that have been perpetrated by Black Americans. These tensions have further come to light over internal debate within the Asian American community as to whether increased policing should be a demand of the movement. Some Asian American community members have advocated increased police presence in Chinatowns as a key and immediate policy act to help elderly Asian Americans feel more secure; however, Asian American have denounced this suggestion, particularly given the disproportionate harm encountered by Black Americans at the hands of law enforcement and its direct opposition to the demands of the Black Lives Matter movement. In a similar fashion, the $25,000 reward posted by actors Daniel Wu and Daniel Dae Kim for information of the perpetrator of street attacks on elderly Asian Americans in Oakland generated discomfort due to the way this was functionally indistinguishable from placing a bounty on a Black man. Choi, Kulkarni and Jeung unequivocally reject increased policing as a solution to AAPI hate and state that "AAPI community members are the least likely to report hate crimes to law enforcement [and] we are not immune to reports of blatant racism in police department ranks and officers' connections to white nationalism" (2022). For these reasons, many #StopAsianHate activists have directed attention to the need to maintain solidarity with other minority communities, drawing on the history of collective activism between Asian American, African American and Latin American students in the Third World Liberation Front. The visibility of #StopAsianHate, then, is meaningfully situated alongside racial justice movements including Black Lives Matter.

The #StopAsianHate movement continues to develop and evolve. A key limitation of the current representation of the movement has been its failure to account for the needs of South Asians. For instance, there was a relative lack of attention given to the April 2021 Fedex shooting in Indianapolis which claimed the lives of eight people, including four Sikh Americans, and reflects a longer history of South Asians being excluded from Asian American activism and advocacy (Kulkarni, 2021), again highlighting on of the limitations to the current visibility framing of this movement. Additionally, one year on from the Atlanta murders, activists continue to debate what the movement's next goals and agenda should be, from increased community resources (Choi et al., 2022) to focusing on anti-Blackness within the community (Zhou, 2022) and mobilizing the Asian American vote (Zhou, 2022).

Engaging #StopAsianHate in the Food Blogosphere

#StopAsianHate offers a useful case study for further exploring how influencer activism is developing and addressing racial justice. Given the investment of the movement in visibility politics and circulating information, Asian American food bloggers would be seemingly well-positioned to engage with the issue through their digital platform. Additionally, this movement offers a useful counterpoint to #BlackoutTuesday: structurally, #StopAsianHate and #BlackoutTuesday evolved in a similar fashion as a response to the build-up and shock of a series of widely publicized race-based crimes that was coordinated with protest marches and the digital visibility of celebrities which, in the case of #StopAsianhate, included Asian Americans actors such as Daniel Dae Kim, Daniel Wu, Ashley Park, Olivia Munn, Sandra Oh and tennis champion Naomi Osaka. However, empirically, far fewer food bloggers spoke out against #StopAsianHate than those that participated in #BlackoutTuesday: only 7 Asian American food bloggers in this sample acknowledged the #StopAsianHate movement or events in any form, approximately half the number that participated in #BlackoutTuesday. More broadly, #StopAsianHate was rarely mentioned across the food blogosphere, failing to reach the tipping point of visibility that sparked widespread participation in #BlackoutTuesday.

Yet while relatively few Asian American food bloggers engaged in the #StopAsianHate conversation at the peak of its circulation in March 2021, those that did were able to use this hashtag as a starting point for expressing personal and negative experiences of race and racism and to commit to a deeper and more sustained form of engagement in racial dialogue that expanded beyond simple engagement with this hashtag. I focus on a close analysis of the ways that three such bloggers – Andrea Nguyen of *Viet World Kitchen*, the Leung family that authors *Woks of Life*, and Michelle Tam of *Nom Nom Paleo* – incorporated Asian American politics within the context of their existing food blog brands.

Viet World Kitchen

Andrea Nguyen, the author of *Viet World Kitchen*, has attracted a lot of mainstream attention for her food work which centers around Vietnamese cooking. Two of her bestselling cookbooks include *The Pho Cookbook* and *Vietnamese Food Any Day*, and Nguyen's extensive food research and the contextualization of her food within cultural histories has been recognized through a prestigious James Beard Cookbook Award as well as through mainstream media engagements, for instance as a contributor to *The New York Times* and a PBS cooking series, ChefSteps. One of Nguyen's guiding principles as a food writer is to make Vietnamese food accessible but also to provide historical context for this food, both through her personal family recipes as well as through extensive research, and the two aims of her work, as stated on her blog, are to "(1) capture the human connections to food and (2) demystify Asian food without dumbing it down" (Nguyen, n.d.).

As with many food bloggers, Nguyen references her family's personal histories, including her family's escape from Saigon in 1973 (2021j) in order to elucidate the Vietnamese experience in the United States, using this post to point out the traumas of these immigration stories. Referencing a handwritten recipe book that her mother brought with her on this journey, she highlights the cultural and emotional legacies embedded into immigrant food, which bear the weight of the losses and hopes of cultural dislocation. However, in addition to these personal histories, Nguyen adds a commitment to using her platform to showcase the diverse stories and histories behind a range of Asian American foodways and histories. On the *Viet World Kitchen* blog and Instagram accounts, Nguyen features posts including a celebration of Khmer New Year with a history of Cambodian American-owned donut stores (2021h), a feature on the work of Jiab

Prachakul, a Thai artist based in Britain whose work focuses on representations of Asian identity (2021a), a story on the origins of the Yee Food Land Asian grocery store in Arkansas (2021i), and a documentary on the history of Japanese candy shop Fugetsudo in Little Tokyo, Los Angeles (2021g). While pan-Asian food is often a feature of the work of Asian American food bloggers, what is unique to Nguyen's approach is the care with which she contextualizes these stories, highlighting the diversity and specificity of individual Asian American experiences, particularly within less commonly documented regions and histories of the United States. Even though these foodways and histories are presented as distinct and unique, they are woven together on Nguyen's sites to generate a rich tapestry representative of the contemporary Asian American foodscape.

This conscious commitment to, and the politics behind, the detailed contextualization of Asian American foodways is articulated by Nguyen in an Instagram post responding to Gerard's casual and unrepentant appropriation of pho. She writes:

> There are many food writers who, like me, carefully research cultural origins, techniques and language before we hit "publish" on our blogs or "send" to our editors. We're sensitive to our readers and community because our words are our service ... Solid research should be the standard for any type of food writing. Even when I write about Viet food, I look things up and cross-reference (my own peeps can be the harshest critics). Doing good work is about being accurate, culinarily curious, and respectful – not just to a cuisine or culture, but to the people who follow you and rely on your work.
>
> (2021c)

However, Nguyen's political influence also extends beyond discussions of cultural appropriation into more radical and organized activism. She uses her Instagram account to publicize several activist campaigns, including Support Our Chinatowns which was set up in response to the rise in anti-Asian hate crimes in 2021 (2021b), the Minnesota Rice project which featured a line-up of Minnesota-based Asian chefs and restaurateurs fighting racism through "build[ing] awareness about Asian Pacific American stories, foodways, and community empowerment" (2021f), and a virtual dumpling fundraiser, which invites people to host dumpling-making parties to raise money for organizations combating AAPI racism (2021e). These advertised campaigns are complemented by posts that feature resources – including reading lists from people of color, and mainstream news articles that detail the events being discussed – and more mundane acts of Asian American community service, for instance, her "fish sauce price dispatch" where she records and circulates the current prices of various brands of fish sauce at her local Asian grocery store (2021d). This attention to Asian American politics is interspersed regularly within the context of her food work in a variety of ways – nestled within more whimsical and personal posts on food, books she is reading, as well as many posts publicizing her work and projects. In this manner, Nguyen deploys a flexibility to her Instagram content and her ongoing commitment to activism means that activist content does not "interrupt" her feed but rather exists as a natural extension to her contextualized approach to Asian American foodways. That is, her framing of *Viet World Kitchen* as a site for "exploration and conversation on Asian food, cooking and culture" (Nguyen, n.d.) ultimately facilitates a thoughtfulness about how activism on race and food is inevitably intertwined with and inherent to this project. Finally, while much of Nguyen's focus is on the Asian American community, with which there is a logical synergy given the focus of her food work, Nguyen's intersectional approach to political action is actively embraced and publicized through the tenor of her posts. Nguyen was a vocal and prolific participant in Blackout Tuesday and actively advocates for an intersectional approach to Asian American activism, suggesting a consciousness of her role as an opinion leader and her role in championing Black solidarity among the Asian American community.

Nguyen's work demonstrates a powerful model for how political activism, particularly around issues most relevant to the Asian American community, can be deployed within the context of a successful food brand. Nguyen's foregrounding of both her Vietnamese identity and the histories involved in her perspective on food and writing in conjunction with her commitment to spotlighting a diverse range of food stories and histories from other Asian cultures – allow her to speak authoritatively as an Asian American activist even though her professional portfolio remains centered around food blogging and writing. Additionally, her demonstrated commitment to allyship and intersectionality presents a radical and contemporary approach to political action that can be used to inform a wide variety of social justice ideals for digital influencers.

Woks of Life

Woks of Life, authored by the Leung family – parents Bill and Judy and adult daughters Sarah and Kaitlin – is a successful food blog focused on the nuances of Chinese cooking. The blog originates as a way of building ties between the family members as they move and travel between China and the United States, and documenting and sharing family stories that are attached to posted recipes. Self-described as "the online authority on Chinese cooking in English!" (Leung et al., n.d.) much of the work on this blog is positioned towards intercultural familiarity and acceptance through food and there are multiple instances of everyday politics that are presented through this work. The tone and framing of the blog revolves around lifestyle education – the site presents many recipe ideas that are classified as quick and easy weeknight meals, inspirational ways to use up leftovers, and healthy meal ideas. For instance, in recent years many recipes published have focused more on providing vegetarian recipes and meat alternatives, for health and environmental reasons. However, alongside these lifestyle pedagogies is a centering of Chinese American cultural traditions with posts celebrating the mid-Autumn festival and lunar New Year embedded alongside the food blogosphere's routine focus on US holidays such as Halloween and Thanksgiving (Leung et al, 2021e); perfecting the recipe for Char Siu (Leung et al, 2021d); and celebrating the depth and diversity of Chinese and Cantonese foods and recipes, focusing on regional specificity and providing explanations and translations of Chinese foods and techniques (Leung et al, 2022). Asian American foodways are domesticated through home recipes for prawn crackers and egg tarts, and Asian American economies are highlighted through posts that feature tours of bakeries in New York's Chinatown (Leung et al, 2021c) and recommendations for products sold by Asian American retailers. The comments on these posts suggest that this content is effective at resonating specifically with Asian American communities.

However, the Leung family also use their platform to participate in more explicit representational politics, for instance, discussing the controversial Recipeasly app which was publicized by co-founder Tom Redman as allowing users to save their "favorite recipes except without the ads or life stories" (Asmelash, 2021). While this app sparked widespread criticism for seeking to exploit the mostly female labor of the food blogosphere while also ignoring the necessity of blogger's narratives as both search engine optimization and community-building tools, the Leung family highlight the racial dynamics of this controversy, posting a CNN article in which they are quoted criticizing the white colonization inherent to decontextualizing recipes from the cultural histories of food bloggers of color (Leung, et al, 2021a). The Leungs use this controversy to note that the narrative contexts for their Chinese recipes are about meaningful engagement with and respect for cultural diversity and, in doing so, foreground racial politics in the food blogosphere.

The Leungs also use their *Woks of Life* Instagram account to engage in #StopAsianHate conversation by detailing their personal experiences of street harassment and abuse, and the impactful ways that the post-pandemic rise in violence against Asian Americans has personally affected them. They write:

The reality is that in the past couple of weeks, our family has ...

- Looked over our shoulders in public
- Worried about making eye contact with anyone on the street
- Made sure to be on the phone with a family member while walking home at night
- Struggled with the tradeoff between defending ourselves and keeping quiet to avoid potential violence
- Read headlines that leave the motives of attackers open-ended, when they're anything but. (Leung et al, 2021b)

This raw post makes salient the intimate and mundane specter of race-based violence as omnipresent for Asian Americans, rebuking the ways in which the model minority myth downplays this threat. Speaking out about these threats also combats the silence demanded by the model minority myth and helps to build Asian American activism through articulating these experiences and sharing them with a wider audience. Embedding this content within what remains a largely food and lifestyle-focused account alludes to the everyday ways in which this fear and the political realities of race are attached to the quotidian Asian American experience. Further, the Leungs explicitly connect their #StopAsianHate post to Black Lives Matter and white supremacy, urging Asian American communities to be actively anti-racist, contextualizing the racial abuse they experience to the wider problem of structural racism. Through foregrounding racial experiences in this way, and presenting them in conjunction with Black Lives Matter content, they inspire a consideration of race beyond commoditization, demanding that audiences acknowledge that the model minority myth only allows for the precarious and conditional acceptance of Asian Americans in the United States. Accordingly, while *Woks of Life* remains centered largely on food and rarely ventures into explicitly political posts, this account's dedicated focus to detailing everyday Chinese American foodways, geographies and experiences works to build Asian American communities and allows the Leungs to seamlessly pivot toward political activism in response to external events and movements.

Nom Nom Paleo

Nom Nom Paleo is focused on sharing information about the paleo diet, both promoting its virtues and providing a series of easy and inspirational meal ideas for those following this whole food, nutrient-dense diet, which requires major modifications from the Standard American Diet (Tam, n.d.). Michelle Tam, the author of this blog, has received mainstream recognition for this blog as a James Beard nominee and a New York Times bestseller for her first cookbook, *Nom Nom Paleo: Food for Humans.* She has over 480,000 followers on Instagram.

Tam publishes a series of posts that highlight both her Asian American identity and the crimes at the center of #StopAsianHate, such as a post celebrating the Lunar New Year, wearing a shirt featuring the quote "It's an honor just to be Asian" by Asian American actor Sandra Oh, which she uses to reference the increase in hate crimes towards people of Asian descent in the United States in early 2021 (Tam, 2021a). She continues highlighting this issue as she posts in response to the Atlanta shootings (Tam, 2021b), and later as she details the racist street harassment endured by a friend's young son (Tam, 2021c). Given that Tam's brand is not primarily focused on Asian foods or foodscapes – even though at times she does include recipes that are Asian-inspired – Tam nevertheless is able to use her platform to center her Asian American identity, and to share her experiences about the fears of violence against the Asian American community. She also provides explicit connections between her personalized discussions of these issues and activist projects, including links to donate to a project to distribute safety kits to the Asian American community and to share resources on bystander intervention (Tam, 2021b). This activism builds on her participation in #BlackoutTuesday, where she urges action through posting resources for understanding structural racism in America and writes: "it's past time to educate ourselves and our kids, listen with empathy, and be active allies and advocates" (2020). Even though Tam's explicit politics and discussions of Stop Asian Hate do not make themselves visible on her food blog, such commentary is made legible on Instagram through her attention to foregrounding her family and her Asian identity even in ways that are not directly linked to the positioning of her food brand. This discussion of politics becomes effective because it is both centered on her personal experiences, on her explanations that foreground action, activism and identity politics in these posts, and is embedded consistently throughout her Instagram account.

These three examples demonstrate how Asian American food bloggers were able to transform their digital food influence into a broader platform for disseminating political information and resources through defining a political agenda within the scope of their food work. Such examples also present a more optimistic account of how influencer activism might work within the food blogosphere, without necessarily disrupting the commercialized logics of this digital influencer culture, but through building spaces and communities that can be readily directed toward and mobilized around activist agendas where necessary. While it is unrealistic to think that the majority of Asian American food bloggers would have the capacity or inclination to orient their food blogs in this way, these case studies provide optimism for the potential of sustained engagement with racial politics as an organic component of digital lifestyle content.

Best Practices for Asian American Influencer Activism

While influencer activism is a project that continues to evolve, and best practices emerge as a result of the creative labour of individual bloggers within the constraints of this genre, Asian American food bloggers' engagement with #StopAsianHate help elucidate guidelines for Asian American influencer activism, including: 1) providing history and context for Asian American issues, experiences and politics 2) making Asian American communities and coordination visible 3) orienting political awareness toward tangible actions and goals 4) actively championing solidarity with Black and other minority communities 5) creating sustained campaigns that go beyond the trend cycles of digital actions.

Provide History and Context

Providing history and context for Asian American issues, experiences and politics is an effective way of drawing on but moving beyond the individual experiences of Asian American food bloggers. While personal experience is central to the representational politics of documenting underrepresented Asian American experiences and demonstrating the everyday integration of race into domestic routine, these personal experiences are too easily discounted when they are attributed solely to the individual's experience. Individual experiences can be helpful in illustrating the impacts of structural racism in meaningful and affective ways; however, providing an understanding of the history and context of constructs such as the model minority myth and yellow peril ideology is more likely to reinforce the structural impacts of racial oppression, which encompass a variety of different actions and impact many individuals, including those without the platform and influence of food bloggers. While sharing personal experiences is important within both political activism and the food blogosphere, it does not in and of itself support the collective social action required for systemic change. Additionally, within the food blogosphere, where race is so susceptible to the forces of commodification and de-contextualization, engaging with the history and context of the Asian American community is an inherently political act that helps to guard against the appropriation of Asian American culture as well as the dismissal of claims of racism within this community.

Make Asian American Communities Visible

Drawing on food blogs as an activist tool involves explicitly making Asian American communities – and the diversity of experiences and people that comprise this community – visible as a coordinated, political entity. This sense of collective identity is important for building and creating space for Asian American communities in a way that is not organically cultivated by the lifestyle content of Asian American food blogs. Making prominent the intentional community and collective work that is central to Asian American activism generates the potential for recruiting Asian Americans to reclaim their political identity through recognition of shared experiences, particularly when it is appended to the visibility inherent to digital influence. Promoting the visibility of Asian American activism is also a political response to the model minority myth which falsely promises conditional citizenship for the Asian American community that is predicated upon their political silence and assimilation into a white supremacist social order.

Orient Political Awareness Towards Tangible Action and Goals

In theory, one of the generic limitations of influencer activism is its tendency to model virtue signaling without further obligations to engage in political action beyond that. In practice, most food bloggers are well aware of this scrutiny and go out of their way to demonstrate the sincerity of their social justice messaging through discussion of donations, personal actions and links to established activist resources. However, I would argue that effective Asian American activism within the food blogosphere involves modelling actions that go beyond awareness-raising campaigns and/or references to the attention economy and food blogosphere. While sharing resources, personal experiences, and information about structural racism and identity politics can be a good starting point, the next phase of the movement requires compelling action and recruitment, particularly amongst Asian American communities. This is obviously challenging for some food bloggers as it involves intentionally moving off-brand and away from the expertise upon which their digital influence has been built, and may not be a feasible action for food bloggers without a pre-existing level of brand visibility and viability.

Actively Champion Black and Minority Solidarity

The tensions and racism that exist between racial minority groups in the United States have long been manipulated as a way of maintaining white supremacy and, for Asian Americans, has been promoted particularly through the model minority myth. It is clear that Asian American activism cannot succeed without challenging the dominance of white supremacy, and that positive coalition building with racial minorities is central to this goal. Thus, positive Asian American activism in the food blogosphere involves actively seeking out and supporting solidarity with Black Americans, challenging the anti-Black racism that has flourished in some Asian American communities and countering the divisive racial rhetorics that have supported the model minority myth and the racial oppression of both Black and Asian American communities. While this allyship has been articulated most often in #StopAsianhate materials as Black and Asian American solidarity, the spirit of this messaging suggests the need for coalitions between diverse racial minority groups and consideration of the unique histories and racial positioning between, for instance, Latinx and Indigenous communities within the scope of this activism.

Sustained Conversations on Social Activism

Another common criticism levelled at influencer activism is its tendency to be driven by online trends and fleeting events. Trending online actions, such as #BlackoutTuesday, have been important for authorizing the integration of activist content within the food blogosphere, drawing on a networked show of influence to collectively challenge the notion that political activism has no place within the lifestyle blogosphere. However, it is also true that for influencer activism to be effective it must be sustained beyond those key moments where social justice topics trend in public. This involves regularly incorporating activist content into the food blog brand and consistently demonstrating that activism can be explicitly engaged in conjunction with digital lifestyle content, and that lifestyle – particularly for Asian American food bloggers – is always political.

Adhering to these best practices is not necessarily possible for all Asian American food bloggers – it is far easier (and less risky) for bloggers who are already well established to redirect their digital platforms toward social issues that may alienate a commercialized following. It also requires an ongoing portfolio of digital content to be able to intersperse activist content without completely reorienting the direction of a food blog. It may also be well beyond the scope and intention of individual food bloggers to tackle this project of identity politics, particularly given the fact that food blogging is often enacted as a livelihood and how research has documented the specific vulnerabilities of and abuse directed toward Asian American women bloggers. However, as the Asian American food bloggers studied in this chapter demonstrate, individual bloggers do have the potential to direct the food blogosphere thoughtfully toward a more racially conscious and socially progressive understanding of lifestyle, and their collective efforts have slowly but surely shifted this digital culture toward a greater consciousness of the racial politics and implications of everyday lifestyle routines.

Conclusion

Documenting Asian American food bloggers' racial activism on Instagram – and the ways in which these posts may be groundbreaking for public dialogue on race – is not to say that these posts are uniformly accepted by followers of these accounts. While most comments posted in response to the Woks of Life #StopAsianhate post were positive, generating both visible communities of support around sharing experiences of structural racism and perhaps emboldening more bloggers to share similar experiences, other comments aired a variety of racist commentary. One commenter writes: "10 white people were just killed by a Syrian immigrant. White hate must end (ac_3825, 2021)" while another posts a string of racist comments:

> Race baiting!!! It wasn't Asian hate! A pervert shot eight sex workers … . You must not read the news you should not be spreading this propaganda it's dividing, the press conference by the arresting officer specifically stated it was not a race hate crime (Ronseamon, 2021);

"I follow you for food – not politics. Stick to what you know" (Ronseamon, 2021); and

Though black people comprise 13% of the population – They committed 27.5% of all violent crimes against Asian Americans in 2018 While whites comprise 62% of the pop. they commit 24% of crimes against Asians But please tell me how white supremacy is the issue (Ronseamon, 2021).

The fact that this latter commenter, whose post perpetuated several racist fallacies, also followed the Instagram accounts of several Asian food bloggers highlights the extent to which the commodification of race remains compatible with white supremacist ideologies.

While such racist commentary was not necessarily the primary response to #StopAsianHate posts, they serve as a reminder of two key things: first, the dismissive responses to legitimate and intimate claims of racism that Asian Americans face, with the comment "I follow you for food – not politics" simply an indication of the civic ostracism of the Asian American communities, whose qualified acceptance into white supremacist society is contingent upon their adherence to model minority behavior, and service through, in this instance, the self-commoditization and translation of culinary pedagogies. Second, the precarity and vulnerability of Asian American food bloggers, whose digital influence is outwardly threatened by consumers when they dare to voice their political opinions, amounting to threats to their livelihoods and mental health. The culture of trolling food bloggers and the vulnerabilities they encounter from audiences as they make themselves vulnerable through personal disclosures, as well as the microaggressions frequently fielded by bloggers of color, already place undue burdens on individual Asian American food bloggers. Moreover, food blogging is often engaged as a hobby, a creative outlet and a livelihood, and within these valid contexts it is unfair to demand that all Asian American food bloggers champion informed and active political goals, particularly as this stance would typically work against their visibility and conditional acceptance within the food blogosphere. Drawing attention to these structural and generic conditions within which Asian American food bloggers are situated underlines the undertaking required of individual food bloggers to publish such activist posts.

As influencer activism increases in popularity across the blogosphere, food bloggers continue to find creative ways to use their branded platforms to disseminate social justice messaging. While influencer activism builds on the lifestyle politics with which food blogs have always already been engaged, as the previous chapters have demonstrated, lifestyle politics has been ineffectual at highlighting issues of racial justice. Within the commercialized and aspirational white lifestyle that predominates in the food blogosphere, this problem is exacerbated by the fact that Asian

American participation is structured through the strategic erasure/commodification of race. Within this curated portrayal of "lifestyle," there is limited possibility for engagement with the negative affect and impacts of racism for the Asian American community and there are few avenues for consciously promoting the formation of politically active Asian American communities. #StopAsianHate challenges this understanding of race in the lifestyle blogosphere, as an important moment in the history of Asian American activism that generated mainstream attention in challenging the model minority myth. While Asian American food bloggers, as a whole, did not participate widely in this hashtag conversation through their branded digital platforms, those that did demonstrated a variety of meaningful ways that a deeper engagement with Asian American identity politics could be fashioned within the context of a successful food blog brand. In turn, these bloggers made salient some of the best practices for championing Asian American activism within the food blogosphere and, in doing so, making visible the racial politics upon which the aspirational lifestyle content of the food blogosphere is based.

The work of race-based influencer activism continues to be ambivalently enacted and received in the food blogosphere. However, I suggest that a better measure of progress takes place not through the success of any individual action – whether that be #StopAsianHate, #BlackoutTuesday or #ImmigrantFoodStories – but through a more gradual process of change to the cultures of food blogging. As individual food bloggers advocate for the need to integrate references to institutional politics and social justice to enrich their digital culture, they practice a feminist politics in challenging the common admonishment to "shut up and stick to food," a refrain that is used to denigrate the value and legitimacy of their work and voice. These references to social justice, in the context of Black Lives Matter and #StopAsianHate, are of particular significance for Asian American food bloggers who have struggled to have their racial experiences acknowledged in meaningful and complex ways within the language and logics of food blogging. In the networked and trend-driven blogosphere, focusing myopically on the benefits and drawbacks of any particular hashtag action or individual bloggers risks obscuring a broader perspective of the ways that change is fashioned through smaller, individual actions.

References

@joeynogood. (n.d.). StopAsianHate.Info. https://www.stopasianhate.info/

ac_3825 (2021, March 19). 10 white people were just killed by a Syrian immigrant. White hate must end [Comment on Instagram post] https://www.instagram.com/p/CMkYZ_1pF6K/.

Asmelash, L. (2021, March 5). What it says about us when we want a recipe but not their humanity. *CNN.* https://edition.cnn.com/2021/03/05/us/recipeasly-food-blog-recipes-trnd/index.html

Cheng, A. A. (2021, February 21). What this wave of anti-Asian violence reveals about America. *The New York Times.* https://www.nytimes.com/2021/02/21/opinion/anti-asian-violence.html

Choi, C., Kulkarni, M., & Jeung, R. (2022, March 16). One year after Atlanta shootings, why we're still struggling with anti-AAPI hate. *Time.* https://time.com/6157617/atlanta-shootings-why-were-still-struggling-with-anti-aapi-hate/

Chow, D. (2021, March 17). Why you haven't heard from us, *Medium.* https://dianatchow.medium.com/why-you-havent-heard-from-us-df274856b0a6

Crenshaw, K. (2016, October). *The urgency of intersectionality.* [Video]. TED. https://www.ted.com/talks/kimberle_crenshaw_the_urgency_of_intersectionality?language=en

Guardian Staff. (2021, March 18). Georgia officer condemned for saying Atlanta shooter was 'having a bad day'. *The Guardian.* https://www.theguardian.com/us-news/2021/mar/17/jay-baker-bad-day-t-shirt-atlanta-spa-shooting

Jackson, S. J., Bailey, M., & Foucault Welles, B. (2020). *#Hashtag Activism: Networks of race and gender justice.* MIT Press.

Kulkarni, S. S. (2021, April 24). South Asians are Asians too. When will our racial reckoning be? *Ms.* https://msmagazine.com/2021/04/24/south-asian-racism-fedex-indianapolis-sikh-shooting/

Leung, B., Leung, J., Leung, S., & Leung, K. (n.d.). About. *The woks of life.* https://thewoksoflife.com/about/

Leung, B., Leung, J., Leung, S., & Leung, K. [@thewoksoflife] (2021a, March 6). If you're interested, check out this article (link in bio) on CNN about the importance of recognizing the individual creators [Photo]. *Instagram.* https://www.instagram.com/p/CMC8NbRl5r8/?hl=en

Leung, B., Leung, J., Leung, S., & Leung, K. [@thewoksoflife] (2021b, March 19). Image credit: @Kimsaira The reality is that in the past couple of weeks, our family has … Looked over our shoulders [Photograph]. *Instagram.* https://www.instagram.com/p/CMkYZ_1pF6K/

Leung, B., Leung, J., Leung, S., & Leung, K. [@thewoksoflife] (2021c, September 8). Let's take a trip to Fay Da bakery and Tai Pan bakery in Chinatown! Spoiler alert: we bought way too [Video]. *Instagram.* https://www.instagram.com/p/CTiVlIwAzLi/?hl=en

Leung, B., Leung, J., Leung, S., & Leung, K. [@thewoksoflife] (2021d, September 17). Char Siu BBQ Roast Pork: Our #1 Recipe of all time! After our HOMEPAGE, the #2 page—and #1 recipe [Video]. *Instagram.* https://www.instagram.com/p/CT599eTgAjf/?hl=en

Leung, B., Leung, J., Leung, S., & Leung, K. [@thewoksoflife] (2021e, September 21). The Mid-Autumn Festival is tomorrow! After Lunar New

Year, it's the second most important Chinese holiday. It's a time [Album]. *Instagram*. https://www.instagram.com/p/CUDDlWZrsrO/?hl=en

Leung, B., Leung, J., Leung, S., & Leung, K. [@thewoksoflife] (2022, February 24). Do you know the 8 great cuisines of China? Each cuisine represents a certain region: 1. Lu Cai – 鲁菜 2. Chuan Cai. [Photograph]. *Instagram*. https://www.instagram.com/p/CaV6R6erry1/?hl=en

Nguyen, A. (n.d.). About Andrea Nguyen. *Viet World Kitchen*. https://www.vietworldkitchen.com/about-andrea-nguyen

Nguyen, A. [@andreanguyen88] (2021a, February 7). It's hard to view art IRL these days but I started this morning with "Night Talk" by @jiab_prachakul. She's Thai, [Photograph]. *Instagram*. https://www.instagram.com/p/CK9Qyanj3T7/?hl=en

Nguyen, A. [@andreanguyen88] (2021b, February 13). Lunar New Year is about hope and building bright futures, especially for our communities. An article @nytimes on Bay Area [Album]. *Instagram*. https://www.instagram.com/p/CLNgXhDBNvV/

Nguyen, A. [@andreanguyen88] (2021c, February 24). I've been on deadline or in my kitchen working, and when I came up for air, some folks asked me [Album]. *Instagram*. https://www.instagram.com/p/CLqJd3JjJvw/s

Nguyen, A. [@andreanguyen88] (2021d, March 2). Fish sauce price dispatch from H Mart. [Video]. *Instagram*. https://www.instagram.com/p/Cak-OWjrZrH/

Nguyen, A. [@andreanguyen88] (2021e, March 25). Dumplings can heal. Check out this virtual dumpling fundraiser being organized by @mybfisgf and join in! #unityisstrength #stopasianhate #asianamericansmatter [Photograph]. *Instagram*. https://www.instagram.com/p/CM1ETbJDiAW/

Nguyen, A. [@andreanguyen88] (2021f, April 8). Check out "Minnesota Rice"! Twin Cities APA chefs, bartenders and restaurateurs are definitely not "quiet good Asians". They have a [Album]. *Instagram*. https://www.instagram.com/p/CNYkMxhhLw_/

Nguyen, A. [@andreanguyen88] (2021g, April 14). Today's Asian American food find — a wonderful documentary about @fugetsudo — a sweets shop in downtown Los Angeles' Little Tokyo. [Album]. *Instagram*. https://www.instagram.com/p/CNn9a4fD7HF/?hl=en

Nguyen, A. [@andreanguyen88] (2021h, April 15). Khmer New Year started today (4/14) and goes until Friday. It's celebrated by many Cambodian Americans. If you love [Video]. *Instagram*. https://www.instagram.com/p/CNqWRICho6u/?hl=en

Nguyen, A. [@andreanguyen88] (2021i, April 19). The Asian American experience isn't all about the coasts. Yee Food Land is in Little Village, Arkansas. Joe Dan Yee's [Album]. *Instagram*. https://www.instagram.com/p/CN0Rv6YhVoo/?hl=en

Nguyen, A. [@andreanguyen88] (2021j, April 30). The end of April is always bittersweet for Vietnamese refugees and immigrants. Bố Già (old Daddy), 90, emailed this to [Album]. *Instagram*. https://www.instagram.com/p/CORjMHJDnSq/?hl=en

Ronseamon. (2021, March 19). Though black people comprise 13% of the population-They committed 27.5% of all violent crimes against Asian Americans in [Comment on Instagram post https://www.instagram.com/p/CMkYZ_1pF6K/]

Say Their Names. (n.d.). #*Say their names.* https://sayevery.name/about

Tam, M. (n.d.). What's Paleo? *Nom Nom Paleo.* https://nomnompaleo.com/paleo101

Tam, M. [@NomNomPaleo] (2020, May 31). No, I'm not going to stick to food. It's past time to educate ourselves and our kids, listen with empathy [Photograph]. *Instagram.* https://www.instagram.com/p/CA03HnxDWG6/

Tam, M. [@NomNomPalep] (2021a, February 21). Happy Lunar New Year's Eve! This year's holiday is bittersweet for me because we aren't getting together with family and friends [Photograph]. *Instagram.* https://www.instagram.com/p/CLKui-VDFdY/

Tam, M. [@NomNomPalep] (2021b, March 18). I'm sickened, angry, and afraid. The violence and racism against Asians is real. It's getting worse. And it won't stop [Photograph]. *Instagram.* https://www.instagram.com/p/CMi_6mtjDaO/

Tam, M. [@NomNomPalep] (2021c, March 25). Stress baking again. (This is a paleo sandwich bread that will be in cookbook #3. Please don't ask me [Photograph]. *Instagram.* https://www.instagram.com/p/CM0e-rbDUq2/

Yellow Horse, A. J., Jeong, R., & Matriano, R. (2022). Stop AAPI Hate National Report. *Stop AAPI Hate.* https://stopaapihate.org/wp-content/uploads/2022/03/22-SAH-NationalReport-3.1.22-v9.pdf

Zhou, L. (2022, March 15). The Stop Asian hate movement is at a crossroads. *Vox.* https://www.vox.com/22820364/stop-asian-hate-movement-atlanta-shootings

6 Conclusion

> I keep hearing about 'this moment' as being one for people of color to be seen and heard. The skeptic in me wonders how long the moment will last. The optimist in me hopes that the moment will not truly be momentary – that the moments will turn into more moments (2021).
> – Andrea Nguyen, Viet World Kitchen

This study of Asian American food bloggers documents the food blogosphere as a digital culture in which self-representations are structured by dominant postfeminist and postrace discourses, as well as through the conventions, architecture and commercialization of the food blogosphere. These forces work to generate digital self-representations that are overwhelmingly centered on presenting idealized and traditional versions of middle-class, white, heteronormative, cisgender femininity in North America. Overwhelmingly, food bloggers comprise a socioeconomically privileged demographic, a result of the food blogosphere's investment in portrayals of subjects who authentically perform aspirational middle-class lifestyle norms. These performances reproduce the ideals of postfeminist discourse: a girlish yet entrepreneurial performance of femininity is exaggerated by food bloggers, who demonstrate both skilled digital labor in addition to domestic labor, forwarding the notion of an empowered yet pleasure-filled model of creative femininity that resonates across the food blogosphere. Asian American food bloggers assimilate and are overrepresented within this digital landscape and are generally successful at presenting their racial background as a commodity with their blogs by contextualizing and providing assurances of the authenticity of their Asian recipes, the value of which is high in contemporary foodie culture. Analyzing the details and impacts of these structural limitations is central to documenting the critical agency

DOI: 10.4324/9781003302278-6

of individual bloggers – their logical responses to constructing branded, intimate, and ongoing identity performances within the legibility of these cultural constraints, and the points at which they choose to reproduce, subvert and rupture these conventions for political purposes. Furthermore, it is in documenting the history of, and the networked labor of individual bloggers coordinating, these moments that give rise to the malleable blogosphere which evolves and adapts to the broader social and political context. While Nguyen hopes that these "moments will turn into more moments" (2021), I suggest that this moment is already a product of more subtle moments that have facilitated the food blogosphere's more recent shift to race-based influencer activism.

Asian American food bloggers have long performed subtle forms of subversion in their digital identity performances that bring to light the contradictions of postfeminist and postrace discourses. In doing so, their work builds on a history of feminist cultural studies scholarship on the everyday politics of audiences and the subversive meanings that are embedded into women's pleasurable consumption of popular culture texts (e.g. Radway, 1982; Ang, 1985). As this present study focuses on food bloggers who produce these texts, I highlight the ways that postfeminist and postrace subjects engage with these dominant ideologies in their everyday lives. That is, while representations of self in the food blogosphere are limited – focused on exemplary and privileged subjectivity, and stylized identity performances that are measured against a subjective continuum of the fake vs authentic – the logics of these performances are an indication of individual bloggers' critical agency in performing, and at times subverting, the hegemonic norms of these subject positions. The first two chapters explore some of the ways that this subversion takes place through centering the quotidian experiences of Asian American women and providing space for contextualizing familial and domestic narratives, where race becomes apparent not through conspicuous difference but through interweaving racial histories and contexts within the mundane and everyday. Additionally, in the course of their work, individual Asian American food bloggers reveal the failures and contradictions of this subject positioning, which often manifest as ruptures that puncture their digital reproduction of postfeminist and postrace discourses. Such findings reveal that food bloggers are not dupes, but strategic and logical entrepreneurs who calibrate their performances of race and gender according to the commercial parameters of digital visibility that make these performances legible.

At the same time, it is important to note the ways that postfeminist and postrace discourses intersect in the food blogosphere to simultaneously make gender hypervisible and obfuscate race. These findings tend to temper the racial politics possible within the food blogosphere. As has been demonstrated throughout this book, while the food blogosphere has showcased women's intimate and mundane experiences and built strong and supportive communities of women who gather around the exchange of food and lifestyle pedagogies, the commercialized representations of race that appear in the food blogosphere discourage honest and negative dialogue on the ways that structural racism impacts non-white subjects, as content which would likely be unpalatable to the imagined white audience for these texts. As race is imagined as a transferable property and commodity in the postrace language of the food blogosphere, the specificity and nuances of Asian American experiences and perspectives tend to be displaced, indicating the failure to build a specifically Asian American community around these texts. Accordingly, while the structural limitations of the food blogosphere and its commercialization prescribe and amplify certain idealized identity performances, this is not in and of itself the main limitation to the political potentiality of the food blogosphere. Rather, the main barrier to Asian American identity politics lies in the superficial and commoditized ways in which race is presented within the food blogosphere.

In broad terms, the pervasiveness and relative success of Asian American food bloggers, in conjunction with the minimization and coded discussions of race, map onto the model minority myth, where Asian American bloggers are granted conditional acceptance into the privileged white blogosphere in exchange for their silence on racism and social activism. However, discussions of race creep into the narratives and recipes of food bloggers. Where Asian recipes are so richly contextualized through family histories and geographical specificities, there is a depth to the portrayal of Asian American foodways and recipes that is difficult to locate in mainstream food media. Asian American femininity is also presented as routine within these representations of the mundane and domesticity, appealing to ideas about the everyday ways in which race is imbricated in quotidian life for Asian American women and generating a meaningful set of representations in the wake of mainstream Western media's limited and offensive use of Asian stereotypes and caricatures. There is ample evidence that, even though such content is not specifically directed toward Asian American audiences, such representations nevertheless resonate in a meaningful way for this community.

This book has also charted the more striking ways in which the food blogosphere has begun to explicitly incorporate racial justice content through engagement with hashtag activism and the Black Lives Matter and Stop Asian Hate movements. The shift from a largely apolitical to more actively engaged food blogosphere demonstrates its porousness and malleability as the spontaneous yet networked contributions of individual bloggers work to shape this digital culture over time in ways that are highly responsive to the broader social and political landscapes, as was seen in the ways that #BlackoutTuesday and #StopAsianHate were featured in the Instagram accounts of Asian American food bloggers. While influencer activism has been the subject of much skepticism and criticism in mainstream commentary, my analysis of #BlackoutTuesday and #StopAsianHate suggests that food bloggers participated thoughtfully and were active in demonstrating that their engagement was not fleeting or superficial. While discussions of race and structural racism were enacted problematically at times, the critical mass and visibility of #BlackoutTuesday constituted a rupture to the churning blogosphere that authorized the inclusion of political content and, specifically, the frank discussion of race and structural racism. This moment then paved the way for #StopAsianHate content to be published and, even though this movement did not attain the same critical mass in the food blogosphere, there is evidence that this content was profound for some Asian American food bloggers and audiences, providing an outlet to share and rally around personal experiences of racism and for linking these experiences to established activist organizations and resources.

The Asian American food bloggers that have the community standing to 'risk' speaking out on political and social issues are outliers: they are highly established and successful bloggers who have the ability to insure their brands and livelihoods against any adverse impacts of their political statements. However, even though they may be in the minority, their visibility and leadership within the hierarchical food blogosphere nevertheless expands their reach and sets a precedent for other food bloggers and their digital content. In the same ways that the spontaneous yet networked labor of individual food bloggers have solidified the conventions of this genre, the blogosphere becomes malleable through the efforts of individual food bloggers to push the boundaries of what is acceptable in this digital culture. Whether these changes to the food blogosphere evolve gradually over time, or through small and intense ruptures, the malleability and sprawl of the blogosphere is the source of its political promise.

While at any singular point in time the content on Asian American food blogs may be interpreted ambivalently in terms of its presentation of Asian American femininity – structured as it is within commercial considerations, postfeminist discourse and generic conventions – exploring the trajectory of the food blogosphere over the past two decades results in a less ambivalent evaluation of the political possibilities of these texts. It is apparent that the food blogosphere has transformed greatly since its inception in the early 21st century: what began as an amateurish and aesthetically ordinary arena for sharing daily thoughts and recipes has transformed into a lucrative and professional digital food content arena. Successful food bloggers are often invited to contribute to mainstream media – for instance, the current sample has collaborated with the Food Network, Food 52, PBS, and Bon Appetit – and the quality of content, styling, photography and recipes is equivalent to these commercial media outlets. While it is true that this increase in professionalization and commercialization of the food blogosphere has greatly increased barriers to participation and visibility – as an excess of cultural capital, skills and resources are required to become established in this saturated culture space – it has also heightened the food blogosphere's responsiveness to trends, community and digital influence, all of which have been central to orienting the food blogosphere toward integrating racial justice content. Within this hierarchy, prominent Asian American food bloggers who have labored to demonstrate the personalized experiences and vocabulary crucial to articulating structural racism and the Asian American experience have shaped trends that authorize political activism around critical understandings of race. Moreover, the food blogosphere's spread to social media platforms such as Instagram has been central to bloggers' participation in #BlackoutTuesday and #StopAsianHate, given the ease and temporality with which intertextual and more personalized information can be incorporated, without needing to maintain strict aesthetic and logical consistency with the food blog brand. A recipe post and a post about activism can be neatly separated on Instagram, whereas discussions of activism on a food blog post would require contextualization within a recipe. Posting on Instagram has also allowed bloggers to participate in networked hashtag activism that originates and extends beyond the food blogosphere. That is, over time it is possible to see how, through individual efforts, the food blogosphere has been reshaped and spread across platforms to push back against limitations and to center the visibility and political action of Asian American women.

The Asian American food blogosphere is built upon a dyad of visibility and invisibility that makes certain topics, identity characteristics, narratives and labor more or less apparent, in a manner that is reminiscent of the operation of the model minority myth. The model minority myth at once obfuscates the significance of race for Asian Americans, suggesting that their assimilation into privileged white cultures makes their race insignificant to their social success and mobility, even while their racial difference is maintained as the grounds for civic ostracism. This play on racial visibility and invisibility is mapped in the food blogosphere. Visibility – and its accompanying financial viability – for Asian American food bloggers is highly predicated upon their ability to successfully perform their identities within the logics of postfeminist and postrace discourse. The resulting commodification of race tends to make more profound racial experiences – and structural racism – less visible. This leaves less room for the visibility of the ways in which experiences such as racism, melancholy and alienation are written into the mundane experiences of Asian American women. However, visibility is also determined by the audience and what they are searching for. This book has documented many instances in which Asian American audiences have selectively made themselves visible as a community through their meaningful identification with content in the food blogosphere. Additionally, 'ruptures' deploy hypervisibility to focus on the contradictions and limitations of postfeminist and postrace discourse. The need to continuously perform visibility in the churning blogosphere has created the conditions for networked change and activism in the malleable Asian American food blogosphere.

References

Ang, I. (1985). *Watching Dallas: Soap opera and the melodramatic imagination.* Methuen.

Nguyen, A. [@andreanguyen88] (2021, October 20). I keep hearing about "this moment" as being one for people of color to be seen and heard. The skeptic [Album] *Instagram* https://www.instagram.com/p/CVNxh4ilZAz/

Radway, J. (1982). *Reading the romance: Women, patriarchy, and popular literature.* University of North Carolina Press. 10.5149/9780807898857_Radway

Appendix

The sample of blogs analyzed for this study is drawn from Asian American, women food bloggers who were Saveur Award finalists between 2009–2019. As very few bloggers publicly identify themselves as Asian American, this sample of blogs reflects a wide net cast in defining Asian and American, with blogs that include people of East, South-East and South Asian heritage living or having previously lived in North America. This includes bloggers who are mixed-race, blogs that are authored by more than one blogger (at least one of whom is Asian American), and bloggers with connections to the United States and Canada.

Table 1 List of food blogs in sample

	Blog Title	Author	URL
1	My Name is Yeh	Molly Yeh	http://mynameisyeh.com/
2	Manger	Mimi Thorisson	http://mimithorisson.com/
3	Nom Nom Paleo	Michelle Tam	https://nommompaleo.com/
4	Hummingbird High	Michelle Lopez	https://www.hummingbirdhigh.com/
5	Omnivore's Cookbook	Maggie Zhu	https://omnivorescookbook.com/
6	Two Red Bowls	Cynthia Chen McTernan	https://tworedbowls.com/
7	Woks of Life	Bill, Judy, Sarah & Kaitlin Leung	https://thewoksoflife.com/
8	Constellation Inspiration	Amy Ho	http://www.constellationinspiration.com/
9	Wild Wild Whisk	Trang Doan	https://wildwildwhisk.com/
10	Viet World Kitchen	Andrea Nguyen	https://www.vietworldkitchen.com/
11	In a Half Shell	Julie Qiu	https://www.inahalfshell.com/
12	Make It Dough	Hannah Dela Cruz	https://makeitdough.com/
13	Binjal's Veg Kitchen	Binjal Pandya	http://binjalsvegkitchen.com/
14	Monica Bhide	Monica Bhide	https://monicabhide.com/
15	Spoon Fork Bacon	Teri Lyn Fisher and Jenny Park	https://www.spoonforkbacon.com/
16	I am a Food Blog	Mike & Stephanie Le	https://iamafoodblog.com/
17	The Pancake Princess	Erika Kwee	https://www.thepancakeprincess.com/
18	Desserts for Breakfast	Stephanie Shih	https://www.dessertsforbreakfast.com/
19	Beyond the Plate	Danielle Tsi	https://www.beyondtheplate.net/
20	Indian Simmer	Prerna & Abhishek Singh	https://www.indiansimmer.com/
21	Just Hungry	Makiko Itoh	https://www.justhungry.com/
22	She Simmers	Leela Punyaratabandhu	https://shesimmers.com/
23	Chinese Grandma	Lillian	https://chinesegrandma.com/
24	Pen and Palate	Lucy Madison & Tram Nguyen	http://www.penandpalate.net/
25	O & O Eats	Summer Min	https://www.oandoeats.com/
26	Love, Cake	Samantha Seneviratne	http://lovecommacake.com/
27	Vermilion Roots	Christine Leong Knight	http://www.vermilionroots.com/
28	Hello My Dumpling	Jenny Huang	http://www.hellomydumpling.com/
29	Betty Liu	Betty Liu	https://bettysliu.com/
30	What to Cook Today	Marvellina Goh	https://whattocooktoday.com/

Index

Asian American: activism 21, 56, 57; civic ostracism 82, 83, 106; community 56, 57, 64–6, 67, 69; diaspora 33, 34, 35, 40, 56, 81, 91–92; identity 29–30, 32–6, 39–40, 69; melancholy 34, 116; relative valorization 82
affordances 17, 27, 58, 68
authenticity 2, 5, 6, 14, 40, 41–3, 47, 112
autobiography 1, 5, 27–8, 29, 35

Betty Liu 62, 68
Black Lives Matter 3, 15, 20, 76, 77, 78–87, 93–5, 107, 114
#blackOutTuesday 20, 75–6, 78–87, 92, 95, 98, 100, 101, 107, 114
Bon Appetit 77, 115
brand 5, 6, 15, 20, 30, 107

Chinese Grandma 1, 27, 37, 39–40, 64
commodity, race as 1, 6, 9, 11, 27, 47
Constellation Inspiration 27, 32–6, 66
content churning 2, 17
context collapse 59, 60
cookbooks 4, 27–9, 30, 45
cultural appropriation 29, 40, 52–4, 103, 113
cuteness 14, 33

database 30, 35, 36
database narratives 30–1, 35

eating the Other 27, 40
everyday politics 1, 20, 48, 57, 112

femininity 7, 8, 12, 13, 14, 27, 28, 32
feminist 3, 5, 7, 11, 27–8, 32, 55, 107
food blogs 3, 4, 12; architecture 32–6, 68; community 55, 63, 67; intimacy 61–2, 68, 69; commercialization 5–6, 63–4, 68; narrative 29
Food Network 16, 26, 115
food porn 5
foodie culture 15, 37, 41–42, 43, 53, 77

Girl Meets Farm 26
girlie 14, 33
guerrilla marketing 5

Half-Baked Harvest 52–4, 97
hashtag activism 3, 20
Hello My Dumpling 74, 86
Honestly Yum 74
Hummingbird High 81

imagined audience 59, 63–4
immigrant 28–9
#immigrantfoodstories 74, 107
In a Half Shell 79, 86
influencer activism 20, 21, 102–5, 112, 113
Instagram 6, 68, 76, 78–86, 96–101, 114–5
intersectional 2, 3, 11, 57, 93, 98, 100

Joy the Baker 75
Just Hungry 27, 42, 46
Just One Cookbook 66

Kitchenista 80

Lady and Pups 66

Make it Dough 84
menu 31–2, 36
#MeToo 20, 80
microaggressions 79, 106
model minority myth 10–11, 15, 85–6, 94, 100, 104, 115–6
mommy blogs 55, 69

neoliberal 2, 7
Nom Nom Paleo 79, 81, 96, 101

Oh She Glows 57
optical allyship 78
Orangette 4, 8

performative activism 75, 78
The Pioneer Woman 4, 8, 13, 16
popular feminism 76
postfeminism 1, 7–9, 10, 17, 20, 28, 34, 36, 46, 111, 112
postrace 1, 2, 9–10, 17, 20, 26, 38, 44, 46, 112

racial triangulation 82–3
racism 16, 52–4, 69, 105–6, 116
Recipeasly 99

relational labor 41, 62, 63
representation 1, 2, 6, 7, 8, 9, 11, 12, 14, 15, 16, 18, 20, 39, 111, 113
rupture 2, 8, 17, 18, 21, 44, 46–8, 69, 112, 116

Saveur 2, 14, 18, 26
self-branding 3, 18, 20, 27, 36–7, 41, 44, 47
sister test 60
Smitten Kitchen 4, 8, 68, 75
Southern Foodways Alliance 77
Spoon Fork Bacon 80
Stop AAPI Hate 91, 93
#StopAsianHate 20, 88, 92–5, 96–100, 104, 105–7, 114

Thug Kitchen 77
tiger mom 2, 40
Two Red Bowls 57, 62, 66

Viet World Kitchen 81, 96–8, 111

whiteness 12–14, 17, 28, 29
Wild Wild Whisk 61, 83
Woks of Life 96, 98–100, 105
Women's March on Washington 76

yellow peril 11
#YellowPerilforBlackPower 85

For Product Safety Concerns and Information please contact our EU representative GPSR@taylorandfrancis.com
Taylor & Francis Verlag GmbH, Kaufingerstraße 24, 80331 München, Germany

www.ingramcontent.com/pod-product-compliance
Lightning Source LLC
Chambersburg PA
CBHW051753230426
43670CB00012B/2275